THE KEY

A Modern Tale of Self-Discovery

By Dean Nixon
and Lee Kelley

THE KEY

Copyright 2017 by TurningLeaf Wellness Center

All rights reserved. No part of this book may be used or reproduced by any means, graphic, electronic, or mechanical, including photocopying, recording, taping, or any information storage retrieval system without the written permission of the publisher, except in the case of brief quotations embodied in critical articles and reviews.

ISBN-13 9780986364914
Library of Congress Control Number: 2017914550

Printed in the United States of America

This book is dedicated to the memory of my friend and brother, Greg Barton, and to all those souls out there searching for answers.

Table of Contents

Rock Bottom	1
Focus	5
Acceptance	15
Communication	27
Evidence	39
Faith and Hope	55
Movement	67
Meditation and Prayer	77
Resolution	91

Rock Bottom

———•••———

Sitting in the Barnes & Noble on a cold January day, watching the rain come down, just two days out of rehab, Isaac was thinking how out of place he must look in his shorts and hoodie ducking in to warm up in the bookstore. The smell of the coffee and pastries made his stomach growl, as he walked toward the back of the store.

He found a list of local shelters and asked an employee to use the phone. The person on the other line said he couldn't get in line until 2:00 p.m. He didn't bother grabbing a book, but simply sat on one of the comfortable couches near the back corner of the bookstore.

Other people were sitting around casually reading, but Isaac assumed they probably had somewhere else to go. This was just a stop in their normal day. Maybe they were relaxing, or maybe they were researching a topic of interest. Nothing interested Isaac right then, except maybe finding the bathroom.

In his line of sight was a display of "must-read" historical works, and apparently, the bookstore was currently marketing Benjamin Franklin. There was a classic-style illustration of the man, with a quote superimposed across the whole side of the display: "If you would not be forgotten as soon as you are dead, either write something worth reading or do things worth writing about."

As Isaac stood at the sink in the bathroom, the warm water on his frozen hands brought an amazing sense of relief. He caught his eyes in the mirror, and said, "Empty" out loud. The sound of his own voice startled him.

Twenty-nine years old and so lost. Everything he loved and everyone he cared about was gone. Removed by his own hurt and pain and shame. As his eyes drifted down from the disappointment, he quickly dried his hands and began to prepare for the bite of the bitter cold. When he pushed his hands into the pockets of his old shorts, his fingers felt the familiar object that he had held onto for so long. For some reason, at that moment, it felt different from before. He would normally wear it around his neck, and didn't remember putting it in his pocket.

He pulled out the key his grandfather had given him. It was four-and-a-half inches long, and not like other keys, as it was very old. It was the length of a 20-penny nail with a flat key-like head with the engravings of the branches of a tree. It did not have teeth like a modern key, but a series of small rings of different shapes and sizes. They appeared to be made from different items, such as little gears and flat pieces of metal.

As he held it, a flood of memories rushed in, taking him back to a time when he remembered feeling warm and alive—seeing it around his grandfather's neck, wondering what it might be. He closed his eyes for a moment.

"Grandpa Mac, what is that around your neck?" young Isaac had asked.

"This?" he replied, fingering the key. "This is a very special key, and one day, it will be yours."

Years later, the time came. He could still feel Mac placing it in his hand, and looking deep into his eyes, as if to speak to the only part of him that could hear him.

"This is the key to one of the greatest treasures, men seek it, wise men speak of it, authors write of it, and now you must find it," he said solemnly. As the memories flooded in, Isaac suddenly felt the weight of his despair. He was tired of hating life, of fighting with it. The quote he had read a few minutes earlier now popped back into his head, and he felt a tiny glimmer of hope that maybe he could do something worth remembering, something worth writing about. He stared at the key for a few more moments, then put it around his neck and went to find a phone.

Three rings. Four rings. Five.

Click. Pause. "Hello?"

"Mac?"

"Hello, Isaac."

"Mac, I'm calling about the key."

The phone echoed with a quiet pause.

"Yes?"

Isaac hesitated. "Something—something is different. I felt something. I don't know how to explain it, but it's different."

Mac chuckled and replied, "Well, it sounds like you might be ready."
"Ready?" Isaac was confused.

"Yes, ready to start living life differently from how you ever have before. To be connected in a way that gives you more control, more peace, more confidence than you ever had before."

"Yes, I definitely want that!"

"Well, let's find out," said Grandpa Mac. "Even an old pony can jump through hoops for a cube of sugar."

"Okay…" Isaac replied uncertainly, as he tried to understand the metaphor. "Is there a bus station close by?"

"Yes. Head that way, and there will be a ticket waiting for you in your name," Mac directed. "See you in a couple days."

Focus

———●●●———

Eight hours into the 18-hour bus ride, Isaac nervously looked down at his bus ticket and read, "Isaac Adam McFarland. Destination: Kalispell, Montana. Departure: Boulder, Colorado."

Isaac became aware of the agitation that was boiling up in his chest. His knee was bouncing with the speed of a sewing machine. He found himself chewing on his last finger nail, realizing that they were all starting to become raw. As he turned to look out the window of the bus, watching the flat barren land of Wyoming fly by, the scenery soon became the backdrop for his memories, and the world that he had left behind.

His last substantial meal had been more than a day ago, but several kind strangers had given him a bottle of water and half a candy bar. Although the bus stopped a few times, he mostly slept, and only left his seat to use the bathroom. When the bus finally stopped at the small post office in Kalispell at 11:00 p.m., Isaac walked the two miles to his grandfather's ranch.

He hadn't been up there in almost a decade—the pre-addiction years. He used to love the feel of the place, the big open sky, the natural smell and sounds that one just can't find or replicate in the city. Now it was all just peripheral background, darkness. He was tired, stiff, and hungry, and filled with self-loathing.

Mac had told him where the house key was hidden, and which room would be set up, so Isaac quietly let himself in and went straight to bed. When he woke up, he saw a pair of work boots, new jeans, and leather gloves next to the bed. Then a note with Mac's handwriting: "Get some breakfast and meet me in the barn."

Isaac walked into the kitchen and saw his grandmother. She looked smaller, older, but still the same sweet smile. "Oh Isaac!" she exclaimed, and opened her arms for a hug. He walked quickly across the room and tried to stifle his tears in her shoulder. Nobody had actually been happy to see him in a very long time. She told him to sit, and offered some eggs, biscuits, and gravy, orange juice and coffee. She then left him alone to eat, and said she would see him at dinner. Isaac was so hungry, and gobbled it all up quickly.

Isaac walked out the back door and across the property to the barn. He could see Mac brushing out his horse, a Palomino. The scene looked like a postcard from a former life. Mac had on a light-colored Stetson hat with a pair of tan gloves tucked into the back pocket of his denim jeans.

His shoulders were still wide and strong, as if untouched by age. He had a strong jaw that highlighted his handsome features. No one ever doubted why he was able to win over Grandma. His legs sported a well-worn pair of Tony Llama boots, bone-colored with a tan snake skin toe. Yet the wrinkles around his eyes gave away the fact he was now an older man. For a moment, Isaac was taken back by how white Mac's hair had become.

His thoughts were interrupted by Mac's voice. "Morning. I thought we could ride and talk. You can take that horse right there. You do remember your way around a horse?"

"Of course," Isaac replied. "I spent most of my childhood on this ranch."

"Okay, good. Mount up. I'll lead."

Isaac was more than willing to follow so he could express all the pain he had been holding on to. As they wound through the backcountry, Isaac told his grandfather about the last decade of his life—never getting a break in life, feeling like his parents didn't give him love and support when he felt like he needed it the most, his boss taking advantage of him and not valuing him enough as an employee to overlook his behaviors, all resulting in his addiction.

Isaac continued his story, delving into his relationships never working, because of the baggage and the drama his girlfriends carried and how their parents continually interfered (maybe if they had just minded their own business, things would have worked out!), about his so-called "friends" not understanding true loyalty and how he was now struggling with trust issues, anxiety, and how "fake" everyone in the world is. Isaac described how he made and lost fortunes, how unfair the judicial system is, and finally, how he was tired of being labeled a "druggie."

But Mac could predict almost every word. He had heard it all before. He himself had spent many years in the victim mentality, the "life-is-so-cruel-to-me" mindset. He mostly listened, with an occasional grunt, chuckle, or heavy sigh, noticing that Isaac was so deep in his story that he was not even paying any attention to where they were going.

Isaac continued, as if he were playing an old recording of the same stories that he had shared repeatedly—the same way he had told them at each of the rehabs on his path to sobriety. Some of the stories were so old that he didn't even feel connected to them anymore. He just shared them out of some sort of feeling of obligation to the stories.

Suddenly, his horse came to an abrupt stop. Coming back into the moment, he realized Mac had pulled up and was now leaning forward with his hat in his hand to block the sun. Looking up he said, "Yup, that's long enough." As he sat back into his saddle and reapplied his hat, he looked back at Isaac and said, "Okay, son, your turn. Take us home."

Mac noticed that Isaac still wasn't watching where they were going. He was just following a vague pair of tracks. Before long, the brush became thicker, they crossed a small river Isaac didn't recognize, and the prints became harder to find.

He looked over at Mac, asking with his eyes which way.

They stopped near an embankment. Mac leaned forward on his horse, one hand on the reins and one on the horn. He peered up from under his hat with that knowing grin and said, "I'm just following you, Isaac."

They kept going, and Isaac pointed, "All right, let's get up on this damn hill and let me get my bearings."

If anything, the view from the top made the situation worse, because now Isaac was certain he was lost. He jumped off the horse and put his hand on his hips. Pushing his hair back with his fingers and letting out a long stressful sigh, he admitted, "I think I'm lost, Mac."

Mac grinned again. "More than you know."

Isaac became agitated. "Please, Mac, I know what you're doing. I don't know where the hell I am, and I don't need this right now."

Mac just looked off into the distance thoughtfully, taking his time with any kind of reaction or response.

Meanwhile, Isaac was stomping and kicking dust, swearing and muttering at himself. Can't even get a damn horse through the woods. I'm such a worthless piece of crap.

Mac could feel what was coming; he'd been waiting for this.

When Isaac went to kick a small log, but got tripped up, he fell to his knees and stayed there. His back heaved as he sobbed with his face in his hands.

The horse kept eating at some grass, disinterested in anything that was happening.

Isaac heard the creaking of Mac's saddle, the sigh of the horse as his rider climbed off.

Then he felt a hand on his shoulder. Mac was down on one knee, showing support and creating emotional space for his grandson. No more grin. No more fooling around. No more stoic silence. Just dark brown eyes full of love and understanding. "Now you are ready to talk," he said.

Mac understood that sometimes, people have to be completely lost in order to find themselves. "You spent the last few hours complaining and focusing so much on your past, that you got lost right where you are at, right now," he told Isaac gently. "You see, we humans are peculiar creatures. We are so afraid of being uncomfortable. We tend to focus on how uncomfortable we are, and then we start making decisions from that place. It's no wonder we even move forward at all. You can either keep focusing on the burr under your saddle, or you can just get on getting on."

With that, Mac slowly withdrew himself and Isaac again heard the creaking of the saddle and the sigh of the Palomino under the weight of the rider as he heard Mac ask, "You comin'?" And Isaac obliged.

As the days progressed, the two, and sometimes with Grandma, shared many meals together. Mac was usually quiet, and Isaac usually rambled on (and on) about his life, beginning to feel invigorated with finally getting all this off his chest. More than once, Isaac would make some observation about his life or lack of success, and Mac would pause from eating his food, and ask open-ended questions like, "How's that turning out for you?" or "Is that the same old story again? When's it gonna change?"

Slowly, Isaac began to see his story differently. Or, as Mac called it, "Combing the burrs out of it." Isaac realized the burrs were his victim-based statements that kept him trapped in his negative feedback loop, preventing him from being able to move forward in his life. Isaac began to realize that his fear of discomfort had caused him to be overly focused on avoiding any kind of emotional pain.

Three weeks later, Isaac was out on the property, running some fence and pulling wire. The sun felt good on his face as he felt the gentle breeze bring a tangible relief to his sweaty forehead. Sleep and hearty meals had been good to him. He was feeling strong and he could tell that he had been putting on some weight, in a healthy way. The color was back in his face, and he seemed to have shed 10 years.

Isaac slowly looked back at the last 40 fence posts he put in, and saw the glint of the new wire that he had strung, and began to feel a sense of pride swell in his chest. The feeling of satisfaction was encouraging, and he had missed it. He paused for a moment and pulled off his hat and then his gloves. He wiped his forehead with his sleeve, and when he caught a glimpse of his blistered, weathered, and calloused hands, he realized how much pain he really was in.

It was a subtle, small voice, but somewhere in his mind, he realized, This is what Mac is trying to teach me. I've been focused on the pain, focused on the story. I don't need the pain of the past to drive my future. I just need to focus on what I am creating right now.

From that moment on, the pain changed from an indicator to stop to a reminder of the person he was becoming. He replaced his hat and gloves and picked up the post hole diggers, and with a newfound sense of purpose, he continued to move forward.

Two months later, Isaac had graduated from fence posts to planting alfalfa. Mac brought him over to the tractor and told him to plow some furrows. Isaac again pretended to be confident, but really wasn't. He did a couple of rounds, then he and Mac looked at the crooked lines together. Isaac's instinct was to beat himself up and he instantly heard himself bring the old stories back.

Mac was patient as a horse. "Just pick a fence post and don't take your eye off it."

Once again, Isaac stopped focusing on his shortcomings and applied himself to listening to the counsel of the man he had come to trust. He realized that by focusing on the fence posts, his lines became straighter and his mind became calmer.

After an especially long day, Isaac was sitting on the porch. He felt connected to everything—the creaking chair, the glass of sweet tea, the red-tailed hawk hunting nearby, a sunset the color of cooling lava. He whispered, "Home" to himself.

Just then, Mac walked up and said, "Come on, I want to show you something."

Isaac followed Mac inside through a couple of rooms, through another door into a somewhat-hidden room he did not remember seeing before.

There was a small door on the back wall between some photographs and books. It looked to be an old-fashioned safe of some kind. Mac turned to him and said, "Let me see the key."

Isaac lowered his head, pulled the chain from his neck, and placed the key in Mac's weathered hand.

Mac paused, nostalgic, running his fingers over the keys and pausing at each distinct section. Isaac didn't know what was going on, but could sense the gravity and significance of this moment.

Looking down at the tip of the key, Mac said, "This part was mine." It appeared to be a piece of barbed wire wrapped perfectly around the key without the barb. "I was the last one to use the key. It was created after the war." Isaac remembered that Mac was a World War II veteran.

Mac put the key into the keyhole, opened the door, and reached in. He pulled out an old leather journal with a leather strap made of antler wrapped around the button. He opened it up and thumbed through it. He then began to remove pages, leaving only blank ones.

Their eyes meet, and Isaac said, "Why did you remove those pages?"

"Those pages were my journey. These pages are yours."

Mac gave Isaac back the key, and closed the safe, and they walked back out to the porch. Mac slowly turned to Isaac, put both hands on his shoulders and looked him square in the eyes and said, "Have you learned a lot, son?"

Isaac responded softly, as if he were replaying the last few months in his mind. "Yes."

"There's more if you want it," Mac offered.

With all the sincerity of his soul, Isaac answered honestly, "Yes, please!"

Mac took Isaac by the right hand and shook it, leaving behind a small piece of paper with a name and address. Isaac unfolded the paper slowly and read the name, "Victor."

When Isaac was getting dressed to leave the ranch, he found a note slid under his door. He put it in his pocket, and then read it on the bus to Chicago:

> Dear Isaac,
>
> You can't plow a straight line by focusing on the cow. Pick a post, Son.
>
> -Mac

ACCEPTANCE

---•••---

Isaac took the cab from the bus station; after a short, chaotic ride through the maze of construction and interchanges, he eventually found himself standing outside a restaurant called Vick's Diner in the heart of Chicago.

As he walked into the middle of a busy lunch rush, his senses were flooded with the sound of laughter and conversation, mingled with the smell of hot, greasy food. The atmosphere was alive and bustling, yet warm and engaging. He waited patiently for a break in the line, and then approached the attractive young woman, whose name tag read "Amy," working the register.

"Can I help you?" she asked with a smile.

"Yes, is Vick in?"

"You want chicken?" she questioned, with a look of confusion.

"No, is Vick in?" Isaac emphasized.

With each exchange, it felt as though the diner grew louder.

Amy patiently replied, "Sorry, one more time."

Isaac leaned forward so Amy could hear him more clearly. "Can I speak to Victor, please?"

"He's in the back," she said. What do you need?"

"My grandfather sent me to meet him."

"Okay... Well, why don't you take a seat?" Amy offered. "What's your name?"

"Isaac."

After two solid hours, and the lunch rush was long gone, Isaac grew impatient. Again, Isaac approached Amy. "Is Vick available? Can I speak to him, please?"

Amy hesitated, and before she could reply, Isaac took the key from around his neck and handed it to her. "Please show this to Vick. He'll understand."

Amy looked a little confused, but took the key and went to the back. Sure enough, Vick walked out, and went directly to Isaac, towering over him. Vick was an impressive-sized man. He had shoulders that appeared to be carved out of pure granite, and deep-set eyes with a stern brow. His hands seemed to be the size of Isaac's head, and looked as though they weren't afraid of work. His olive skin presented a short stubble as though he hadn't shaved that day, and his apron wore evidence of the breakfast and lunch rush.

As Vick peered down his nose at Isaac, he held out the key, and said gruffly, "Where did you get this?"

"Mac is my grandfather. He sent me to see you."

Vick then smiled, and without missing a beat, turned to Amy and said, "Get us a couple of cheeseburgers, would you? And some pie." Then he turned back to Isaac. "What are you drinking?"

"A soda would be great!" Isaac answered, relieved.

Vick then led Isaac over to a booth, and asked how Mac was doing. Isaac explained that Mac was still on the ranch, described to Vick in as much detail as possible the beauty and the majesty of the ranch, and then told a few stories about Mac that only Vick would understand. Vick asked about his grandmother and her cooking, saying she was twice the cook he would ever be. The food came out quickly, and Isaac began eating, famished from a day on the bus. Through the laughter and storytelling, the time seemed to slip away.

Although Vick had a certain tough exterior about him, it soon became clear to Isaac that he was kind, friendly, and loved to laugh. And apparently he was also well-liked, because people kept stopping by to wish Vick a good day and thank him for the food.

Soon Amy stopped by to clear the table and Vick asked for the checks. After a few moments, Amy brought back two checks and handed them to Vick, who then handed one to Isaac. As Isaac looked down at his total, $12 without a tip, his heart raced in fear of the embarrassing moment that was about to happen.

He looked up at Vick, and quietly admitted, "I don't have any money. I'm so sorry."

"I know," Vick said quickly, without judgment. "That's why you need to be here at 6:50 a.m. tomorrow. Your shift starts at 7:00. You're going to need money for this journey."

He handed the key back to Isaac. He then told Isaac he could stay in the small apartment above the restaurant for $50 a week. Much cheaper than a hotel, Isaac thought.

Isaac walked up a narrow set of stairs to the apartment. It had the look and feel of a place Victor might use if he had to work late. There was a bed, a sink, a toilet, a hot plate, and a mini fridge. It was enough.

The next morning, Isaac was outside in the front of the restaurant before seven, when Amy walked up. Isaac noticed her sweet, slightly crooked smile, revealing a small glimpse of her white teeth.

"Good morning!" she said brightly.

"Good morning," Isaac replied awkwardly.

Amy then unlocked the front door and began to turn on the lights. She went behind the counter and grabbed Isaac an apron, and led him into the dish room. There were plastic carriages and a sprayer. Amy showed him how to fill the racks and use the large dishwasher.

Isaac could feel the instant attraction toward her, and began flirting with her while trying to play it cool. "I think I can handle the dishes," he said teasingly, but with confidence.

"Okay, if you say so," she smiled. "It gets pretty busy back here."

A few other employees made their way in and prepped their areas. The breakfast rush was not too busy, and Isaac kept up fairly well with the dishes that came back.

However, the lunch rush was intense, and within a half-hour, the buckets of dishes were piling up all around him. As he scrambled to wash off the dishes and load the washer, he was shocked by all the wasted food.

At one point, a tub fell over and a couple of plates broke into pieces. Vick happened to be walking by at that very moment, and said, "Hey, that's coming out of your check! Five bucks a plate."

"Hey, it wasn't my fault!" Isaac protested. "It was stacked too high and just fell."

"You're the dishwasher. It's your responsibility."

Isaac broke a few more, and tallied in his head how much he owed: $20 for the broken plates, and $12 for two meals so far.

After the lunch rush, Vick and Isaac sat in a booth near the front windows.

Vick said, "Amy, bring us a couple more burgers and fries please, and a couple of chocolate malts." He looked at Isaac. "You like malts?"

Isaac was still complaining about the servers stacking the dishes too high, and being charged for something that wasn't his fault.

Vick sat back, looked at Isaac, and said, "So what? Now what?"

Isaac became confused, shaking his head, and said, "Excuse me?"

"So some dishes broke and you have to pay for them. So what are you going to do about it?"

"That seems unfair," Isaac huffed.

"Life is fair because it's always unfair," Vick shot back. "So what? Now what?"

"It sounds like if I want to keep my job, then I will have to suck it up and pay for them."

"Well… You don't have to," Vick responded.

"Okay, okay. I'll pay for them!" Isaac retorted with an angry look, which Vick diffused with his big smile.

"Look, kid, I'm just trying to make a point. All kinds of stuff happens in life, right?"

"Yeah, of course."

"Okay, well, each time something happens, you have a choice," Vick continued. "You can choose to be a victim and feel sorry for yourself and keep telling everyone how unfair it is. Or, you can ask yourself, 'So what, now what?' You might not be responsible for stacking dishes the way they were, but you are accountable for what happens to the dishes when you're on shift. And you are definitely accountable for how you react."

Vick paused to take a bite of his cheeseburger and a long sip of the malt. He went on, "So you can get mad and play the victim. This is like giving your power away, because the weather, the customers, or the laws of gravity that made the dishes fall are all against you. Or, you can just say, 'So what, now what' and decide what you can do about it, what you can control, what you can learn from it. And let me tell you something—there are only three things in this entire world you can control."

"And they would be?" Isaac responded with a slight hint of sarcasm.

"You have control over how you think, how you feel, and how you act. That's it!" Vick said emphatically, as he slapped his hand on the table hard enough to make the silverware jingle and heads turn around. "So you might as well learn to let all the rest of it go, instead of carrying it around all the time. That chip on your shoulder is turning into a crack in your character."

Vick smiled and leaned over and put his hand on Isaac's shoulder as if to say, "We're done; it's time to let go."

Once again, Amy returned to the table with the check. Isaac noticed her gentle manner and was grateful for the comforting smile. Isaac's bill came to $15 with the malt. He looked up at Vick. "You gotta be kidding me. Three bucks for a malt?"

Vick grinned. "But totally worth it… right?"

After a couple weeks of working dishes, Isaac moved on to the grill. Yet again, Isaac was feeling cocky about his abilities, but the dinner rush started quickly and didn't let up. The order tickets were backing up and servers were yelling changes at him like, "Hold the onions on that last ticket."

Before long, Isaac was losing track of orders and started burning burgers. As Vick passed by, he would simply say, "That's 5 cents a patty." Isaac began to feel his face become red and flushed, and before long, he couldn't control his thoughts and the voice in his head became self-deprecating and abusive.

A half-hour later, Isaac was highly agitated, and now 20 tickets behind. He then saw Vick heading his way again, and braced himself. But Vick calmly said, "I got this," and took over.

Isaac watched as Vick handled the grill calmly, flipping burgers and timing them with dipping fries in the grease. He began to plate the burgers, along with the fries, and placed the order ticket under the plate before yelling, "Order up!"

Even though people were still yelling and Vick still had to look up to read orders and make fast decisions, Isaac was amazed that he was completely calm and balanced. He noticed that Vick was present and engaged with what he was doing, he prioritized what he could do quickly, and identified what could wait. He calmly, yet confidently communicated with the wait staff and asked for clarification without getting frustrated. Before long, the backlog of tickets was all caught up. He then stepped back and let Isaac take over. Isaac took a deep breath and softly whispered to himself, "So what? Now what?" With that etched in his mind, Isaac was surprised at how much better he performed for the remainder of the rush.

Sitting down with Vick to eat later, he complimented Vick on his finesse on the grill and apologized for getting hotheaded. Vick asked, "You did better, right? What changed?"

"Well nothing changed, really. I just got a little more comfortable back there after watching you."

But Vick asked again, more emphatically, "What changed?"

Isaac paused and thought for a moment. For once, he didn't reply with the quick and easy answer.

"Well, I guess the only thing that changed was me."

Vick nodded with the smile that expressed the pride of a teacher. Then he explained that control only exists in chaos and vice versa.

"Just because we are in control of ourselves in a certain situation, that doesn't mean there is an absence of chaos. Even in quiet moments, in the stillest part of the night, chaos can rage in our minds. Once we begin to control the inner chaos, the outer chaos becomes more manageable."

"Inner chaos?" Isaac repeated, confused.

"Yes, your inner dialog, that negative self-talk. I can see it in your eyes when it happens."

"How do I manage the inner chaos?" Isaac wondered.

"By setting boundaries with how you think about yourself and how you talk to yourself," Vick answered.

A few weeks later, Isaac was moved again—this time, to work the register. And now Amy was his teacher. Isaac became acutely aware of his concern about impressing her. Despite his frustration, and even being yelled at by a couple of customers, Isaac could tell that the small adjustments that Vick was teaching him were paying off.

Isaac and Amy shared a few meals and deep conversation, and he had never felt more open and honest in his life. He shared with Amy about his experience on the ranch with Mac how he realized that he had become lost by focusing on his past and stayed lost by trying to avoid the pain of the future. He talked about the blisters turning to callouses and said he finally understood that dealing with the pain gave him the ability to cope and he recognized his coping skills were now his "emotional callouses."

They laughed about the dishes and burnt hamburger patties and mused over Vick's ability to always stay positive.

Days slipped into months, and Isaac's friendship with Amy deepened.

One day, the two were eating and laughing when Vick walked up and interrupted, looking at Isaac. "You paid off your tab and I'm sure you saved up quite a bit. It's time for you to unlock the next door, my young friend. Follow me."

Vick led Isaac into the cellar, and then to a hidden door in the corner behind a large rack of supplies. The cellar smelled like boxes and dry goods, and the silence was punctuated by the compressing of the soda machines every couple of minutes.

Vick asked for the key, and then paused to look at it, just as Mac had done. Vick ran his fingers across the key, as if remembering a ghost from the past. He smiled and unlocked the door. Isaac's mind whirled with anticipation with what might be inside. Slowly, Vick reached in and pulled out an old worn English-Italian dictionary.

Vick looked deep into Isaac's eyes. "This next step is an important one for you specifically. Everything your grandfather and I have given you has prepared you for this. Hugo is your next teacher. He saved my life many times. Treat him with respect."

As Amy dropped him off at the terminal before her shift, Isaac expressed how nervous he was. "I never have been out of the country before." At that moment, he realized that he felt like he could tell her anything. She gave him a hug across the seat and whispered, "You'll be fine. We'll be here when you get back."

As he closed the door behind him, he realized he was heading to Italy for a couple of months, and it took almost all of his savings to cover the airfare. He had not spoken to Mac since he left Montana, but Vick made it clear that this was the next step in the journey.

As he walked away from the car, Amy yelled, "Isaac, wait!" She was running toward him, and for a moment, he thought (and hoped) she was going to kiss him.

Instead she handed him a brown paper bag. "Here. Lunch for the trip."

On the plane, Isaac read the note he had found from Vick that morning:

Dear Isaac,

Remember, you can't control the whole world. You can only control your perspective. You can learn to accept the rest.

Don't let the chip become a crack.

Safe travels.

P.S. This prayer got me through some dark days:

> "God, grant me the Serenity
> to accept the things I cannot change,
> the Courage to change the things I can,
> and the Wisdom to know the difference."

-Vick

COMMUNICATION

―――――――――――――― ●●● ――――――――――――――

During the long flight and several plane changes, Isaac struggled to control his thoughts. He would sometimes remember Vick telling him how Hugo had saved his life. He imagined that Hugo must be a big man in order to save Vick. He played out scenes in his mind on what it might have been like during the war.

Isaac landed in an airport near the Italian city of Messina.

Vick had told him there would be a driver waiting, and sure enough, there was. The small, older Italian gentleman holding a sign with his name on it smiled as their eyes met.

Isaac walked up and put his hand on his chest and said, "I'm Isaac."

The driver smiled and nodded from beneath the brim of his felt hat and started walking. Confused by the lack of conversation, Isaac paused and then followed him.

Into the back seat of the small Fiat, Isaac quickly jumped as the driver began to speed away.

He pulled out the dictionary and tried to ask a few questions about how long the drive would take. The driver only waved his hand dismissively as he was trying to navigate through chaotic traffic. Isaac soon realized that trying to have a conversation with the driver at this time was a futile exercise, and finally sat back, let it go, and tuned into his surroundings.

It was a beautiful port city, with lush green rolling hills, narrow streets that wound the small villas, and steep cliffs. Isaac was amazed by the history that each of these structures must have contained. Porcelain white, with orange tile roofs. As he peered into the bay, he saw fishing boats and cruise ships bobbing around in the clear blue water. The white sands of the beach seemed to be beckoning him.

They drove though winding streets with many palm trees and thick green foliage and canopies covering the streets. Finally, they rounded a corner and a beautiful villa came into view. The car came to a stop as Isaac peered out at blue doors, shutter windows, and balconies.

The driver motioned to Isaac to grab his belongings and follow him as they walked up the iron-railed stone steps. The driver soon knocked on the door of the villa and carefully pushed the door open, announcing himself and motioning to Isaac to follow.

There was an older woman in the foyer, along with a young man. She did not speak English, but her eyes and body language were very welcoming and kind. The young man explained that she, Maria, was Hugo's wife, and he was their only son, Paolo. He showed Isaac to his room. It was simple; it had a small metal-framed bed with a tan-colored three-drawer dresser, a small rack in the corner for his clothing, a quaint little writing table with a lamp and a wooden chair close to the bed; and a window with sheer drapes on a far wall. Isaac pulled the drapes back and felt the softness in his hand as he peered out to the beautiful bay. *I wonder if they think I am somebody special*, he thought.

The bed linens and pillow smelled of fresh air as Isaac laid back to rest for just a moment. The faint sound of the ocean and the cool breeze were the perfect space for a tired traveler to drift slowly off to sleep. As Isaac slept, Paolo returned to the room and slowly pulled the door closed, recognizing that Isaac needed some quiet rest.

A soft knock came at the door an hour later, and Paolo slowly opened it and entered. With him came the smell of Maria's cooking that filled the air with spices and warmth.

In his broken English, Paolo explained that supper was ready, and that Isaac would be their guest of honor. As Isaac followed Paolo down the hall, he asked, "Will Hugo be joining us for dinner?"

"Yes."

A few minutes later, the family was settling in at the table when in walked the driver, who was greeted warmly and acceptedly by the family. Isaac sat down at his predesignated spot as the guest of honor. As he looked around the table, he realized that if Paolo was their only child, the other eight spots must be extended family or guests. Laughter and conversation filled the room. The scene was warm and inviting, and although Isaac didn't understand a word being said, he recognized that he didn't feel out of place.

After a short prayer spoken in Italian, the food was passed around. Paolo noticed that Isaac kept peering toward the door and soon asked if everything was okay.

"Yes, everything is fine. I was just hoping to meet Hugo tonight."

Paolo smiled, then turned to the family and relayed Isaac's concern to the family in Italian. As the room burst into laughter, the driver stood and with a big grin, said, "Yes, I am Hugo."

Later, Isaac found Hugo sitting out on the balcony overlooking the night lights of the city. The air was cool and smelled of ocean and flowers. Isaac began to apologize to Hugo for his confusion, and expressed that he hoped he hadn't insulted him.

"No need for an apology," Hugo reassured him. "But I am curious at what you were expecting?"

Isaac relayed his daydreams on the plane on the way over and how he had imagined him saving Vick many times. He conveyed that he thought that he would be a bigger man than Victor, and Hugo softly chuckled at the contrast.

Hugo was an average-sized man. Dark hair, almost blackish, thinning on top. What was left was combed over. Dark eyebrows atop brown, warm eyes. A face weathered by time and sea told a story of a man who had seen dark times, yet smile lines that showed that he had never succumbed to the darkness. There was nothing heroic about his features other than the resolve in his eyes.

Hugo softly spoke and said, "There is more than one way to save a man. Physical strength is one thing, but mental and emotional strength is another entirely. It is interesting that you assumed so much and created such a vivid back story in your mind.

"This in one of the main things that truly affects our ability to communicate and understand the world around us," he continued. "Too many times, we make assumptions and then we build a world in our minds around those assumptions. That world is truly the world that limits us, and our limitations become accusations. Accusations we make toward ourselves, accusations we make toward others that lead to the beliefs that our minds fight so hard to hang on to.

Hugo paused for a moment. "I see the fear in your eyes, my young friend," he said to Isaac. "Not that you feel scared right now, but the fear that you carry every day and make decisions from. The fear that you believe is reality, and the reality that you believe defines you. I can tell that there is a gap between who you are and who you think you are. I am intrigued to see which path you choose to follow."

As the magic of the night continued, Isaac's heart was filled with both understanding and questions. He again felt as though time had stopped. The stars and the city lights had become one. The perfumed night and the soft wind all created the perfect moment. Changing the subject, Hugo placed his hand on Isaac's shoulder with a gentle squeeze. "I am looking forward to tomorrow, my young friend."

Hugo explained that he was a captain of a fishing vessel, and he was hoping that Isaac would be willing to lend a hand. Isaac's heart leaped at the idea of spending his days at sea. His imagination began to run, like a dog chasing a ball, as he heard himself think, Be calm, stay in this moment, just be here, tomorrow will come.

As the days and weeks progressed, Isaac felt alive and engaged with the time at sea, smelling the ocean, hearing the waves crash, feeling the mist across his skin, and the sun warming him from the inside out. Hugo's son Paolo became like Isaac's big brother. He kept an eye on him, served as an interpreter, and taught him how to keep his feet from getting tangled in the lines and in the nets.

When they were not out at sea, Hugo turned Isaac over to Paolo to handle the various jobs required to maintain such a beautiful villa. Isaac found himself happily painting, doing simple house repairs, cleaning, and even helping in the kitchen, where he relished the amazing smells of Maria's cooking. When there was downtime, Paolo had endless questions about life in America, and Isaac asked about their culture, the city, and the family.

One evening, while Isaac was sitting with the family for dinner, there was a feeling of excitement in the air. It was a special meal, and he could see that everyone was very excited. Some of Maria's family had traveled more than 16 hours from the Island of Sardinia, where Maria spent her childhood.

The dinner smelled exceptionally wonderful, and Isaac was more than excited to share another amazing meal. Maria came in almost ceremonially, bringing with her a dish covered in an embroidered cloth.

She placed the large dish and placed it on the center of the table, much to everyone's excitement. Hugo gave a meaningful prayer, most of which Isaac was unable to understand. He did, however, pick out a few words that expressed gratitude and love for the family. Maria then removed the cloth as everyone at the table gasped with delight, except for Isaac.

He was totally unprepared for what was underneath, and his face instantly contorted with an expression of shock, surprise, and then disgust. The dish was a cheese that appeared to be covered in maggots. As the cloth was removed, a few of the maggots were disturbed, and launched themselves from their resting place onto the table as the family responded with laughter and excitement.

They were small, white translucent creatures that Maria quickly picked up and quietly placed in a napkin. As she looked up, she caught Isaac's eye as he became immediately aware of the disgusted expression still on his face. Her face dropped. Isaac could tell that her feelings were deeply wounded. She recovered quickly with a smile and a nod, and very gently removed as many maggots with a spoon as she could into a napkin, and retreated to the kitchen.

Isaac self-consciously looked around to see who may have picked up on the exchange. He found Paolo staring at him with hurt and frustration in his eyes, then quickly turning and looking away from Isaac. The rest of the family continued enjoying the cheese, along with the rest of the meal.

Later, in the quiet moments of the evening, Isaac tried to engage Paolo in conversation; however, Paolo was visibly upset. As the only child, he was very protective of his mother. On several occasions over the next two days, Isaac continued attempting to engage Paolo in meaningful conversation, looking for his old friend, his big brother. Eventually, Isaac's patience wore thin and his anger got the better of him. He began peppering Paolo with questions. "Why won't you talk to me? Why won't you look at me? Aren't we friends?"

Finally, Hugo, observing the interaction between the two young men, stepped in. There was a break in the fishing, so Hugo let the boat sit idly. As the waves slapped the side of the boat, Hugo sat both young men down.

"These seas have seen a lot of war. One that I remember vividly, driven by anger and fear. As I have watched the two of you, I am reminded of submarines and battleships. When the battle begins, the submarines close the hatch and dive below the surface. On occasion, they find a battleship and dive deep. The battleship does not know where the submarine may be, but fearing an attack, it will drop depth charges that are perfectly timed explosions designed to crack a submarine like an egg.

"In response, the submarine dives deeper, navigating to find an opportunity to fire a torpedo in return. Both will spend days chasing each other, driven by fear. These ocean bottoms bear testimony of the battled ships and submarines and crews lost at sea."

Hugo paused, and took a deep breath as he turned to face the sun as if to chase the fear away. "But what if it were different?" he asked Isaac and his son. "What if the submarine had found its way to the surface, opened its hatch, and began to communicate? And what if the battleship stopped chasing and dropping bombs, waited patiently, and then spoke?"

Then Hugo paused again, and stared off into the distance as though a memory had somehow caught his eye. "So much loss in this world," he whispered. "So much anger and hate. Mastered by fear."

Shaking his head, he turned to look the young men in the eye. He smiled and said, "It all starts with a question. Not just any question. A question that leads to understanding. It is so easy to be tempted by the questions that wound, like torpedoes or death charges. But instead of questions that are weapons, we use questions that create clarity. Questions like, 'Can you help me understand?' or 'What can I do differently?' The difference between a weapon and a tool is the intention."

Hugo then pulled his fishing knife from its sheath. "Do you see a weapon or a tool?"

"Both," Paolo answered quickly.

Hugo then returned it to its sheath, and said, "Your relationships will depend upon you choosing either weapon or tool. It's time for the two of you to talk."

Hugo returned to the wheel of the boat.

"You hurt my mother," Paolo began the conversation after some silence.

"I know I did," Isaac replied. "I am so sorry. I was just caught off guard. I have never seen anything like that before. I meant no disrespect, and I told your mother so. I told her I was deeply sorry for my conduct. She hugged me and told me it was okay. Now it is your forgiveness that I need."

Paolo smiled and said, "Thank you for respecting my mother, and I do forgive you."

"It's called casu marzu," he explained. "It's a traditional dish from my mother's home, and she works very hard to make it." Paolo then chuckled as he exclaimed teasingly, "Your face looked like this!" They both began to laugh, then embraced, and got back to work.

As the day continued, Isaac began to think about the comment Paolo made about his face; he realized that much of what he has said and what others have said is unspoken. Later, as Hugo steered the ship home, he explained to Isaac, "In Italy, we say more with our hands and faces than we do with our words. We are very expressive people. Every culture is affected by what you call 'body language,' but some are more expressive than others. It is important to be aware of not only your own body language, but also others'. Sometimes crossed arms can imply a closed mind, or sometimes it's just because you're cold!" he laughed.

Hugo then looked Isaac in the eyes, and said, "Become aware of the language that is unspoken, and the world will open up to you."

During the remaining time that Isaac spent in Italy, he began to integrate some of his new tools. By studying people's body language and asking questions for clarity, he began to see this country in a whole new way. His fondness for the family and the people gave him a sense of himself that he had never found before. *I can exist anywhere, as long as I am willing to engage,* he thought with wonder.

The evenings had become a familiar scene. The cool night air, the comfortable conversation, the laughter, and the smells. Hugo leaned close and said, "It is time, my young friend. Follow me."

Isaac rose and began to follow Hugo into the house and into a small back room filled with boxes and old nets and tools. Hugo moved a stack of books on a table and asked Isaac for the key. Just as Mac and Vick had done, Hugo seemed to forget about Isaac for a moment and just took time to examine the key as if casting the lines of his memory back over time, over history. He began running his fingers over to a tiny gear from the handle of a fishing reel.

Hugo opened the door and pulled out an old black-and-white photograph and handed it to Isaac. It was a group of soldiers, some standing and some kneeling, none smiling. Without a word, he pointed at a man on the front left, and then pointed back to himself. Isaac looked between Hugo and the man, and nodded. Hugo pointed to another man, and Isaac stared and then exclaimed "Mac!" He then ran his finger across the back row—"and there's Vick!" Hugo nodded.

Hugo went on, "These men will always be my brothers," and his voice cracked. Isaac put a hand on Hugo's shoulder, for the first time taking the role of comforter.

Hugo reached back into the safe, and pulled out another small photograph and a leather bracelet. The bracelet appeared to be made from a long piece of a leather boot lace. Each end was fastened in a double fisherman's knot in order to be self-adjusting. Hugo slipped it over Isaac's wrist and adjusted it. "In relationships, it takes two to hold things together."

Then Hugo handed Isaac the photograph, pointing to someone else. "This is Ricardo. He is one of the smartest men I know. He has your next piece."

As Isaac scanned the picture, he saw a very handsome young Hispanic man with strong features. He looked up at Hugo. "How will I find him?"

"He is deep in the jungle of Colombia, last I heard. Victor will have his exact whereabouts. You may want to start there."

The very next day, Isaac thanked the family profusely, and then hugged and kissed Maria. As he turned to embrace Hugo, the man paused and reached into his pocket and pressed into Isaac's hand a folded piece of paper. "For later." He then embraced Isaac strongly for half a minute.

Paolo then drove Isaac to the airport. After hugging and exchanging contact information, Paolo said, "We are brothers now."

Isaac was heading back to Chicago to save up some money for the next leg of the trip; it felt a little bit like going home. He was excited to see Amy and share with her all that he had learned and experienced. He was also very thankful to have a job waiting for him.

On the plane ride, he pulled out the note from Hugo, and read:

Dear Isaac,

My young friend, our best conversations are more than just words. Communication requires us to let go of assumptions and not only listen, but see what is being said. The truth lies in the moment, not in the wounds of the past, or the fear of the future.

-Hugo

Evidence

From the moment that Amy picked Isaac up at the airport, Isaac couldn't stop talking. He had so much to tell her. The more he talked, the more he realized that Amy was that safe space for him. She just listened, and at times, he found himself getting lost in her deep brown eyes.

The weeks went by quickly, and Isaac often found himself daydreaming about his adventure. He wanted to be more prepared this time, so he began studying his Spanish/English dictionary during his work breaks.

Isaac began to realize that, for the first time in a long time, he finally felt home. Remembering the old cliché—"Home is where the heart is"—he thought, I must be starting to feel my heart. All the hurt and pain that he had used to guard his heart was beginning to melt away with healing and understanding. His job in Chicago and his little apartment above the restaurant became a real comfort, a foundation on which he could build.

And then there was Amy. He was taking his time and keeping his feelings well below the surface, but he felt something new with her, a real connection.

Take your time, Isaac. Do not screw this up, he often told himself. He was determined to take his time and finish his adventure before he allowed himself to tell Amy how he truly felt. He knew there was so much more for him to learn in order for him to become the man he wanted to be, for himself and for Amy.

Isaac worked hard and became much more adept at the grill. He also enjoyed using his new communication skills at the register, and he didn't even mind stepping in to cover the dishes. He realized he was enjoying everything.

The night before he left town, Isaac took Amy out to dinner to a local steakhouse and the conversation turned to work.

Amy said, "Vick has nothing but good things to say about you lately," Amy said. "And believe me—he's not shy about criticism if he thinks it will help!"

"Oh, don't I know it!" Isaac laughed. "I am going through a big shift, I can feel it, and I appreciate Vick more and more every day. I feel like this was always meant to happen, and I wonder if Mac was just waiting for me to ask for help."

Amy gently tilted her head to the side. "Did you ever ask him? When was the last time you talked to Mac?"

Isaac thought for a moment. "Before I left to Italy. I guess I'm just not used to letting people in my life like that."

"Maybe you can call him before you leave for Colombia," Amy suggested.

The conversation drifted, but eventually came back to Isaac's adventure.

"I can't believe that I've had these amazing mentors spend their time and share their wisdom with me. They are each so patient, kind, and loving, yet they are being really mysterious about why they are helping me. It seems like there is some kind of 'brotherhood' or private oath they all took.

"I don't know, and to be honest, I'm not pushing for those answers. Like I said, I'm just happy to be given the opportunity at this point. I was at a real low just a few months ago, but I've told you that story too many times already."

Isaac smiled self-consciously, and said, "Wow, listen to me, just rambling on. Thank you for just being there when I needed somebody. You have always treated me so kind… now, your turn!"

Amy smiled and held his eyes for a long time. "You are very welcome. And thank you for dinner. Still think you can ice skate faster than me?"

"Let's find out," Isaac said with a grin, as they headed out to a nearby ice rink.

Amy drove him to the airport the next morning, and after a long hug, she kissed Isaac on the check. "Be safe." And once again, she handed him a sack of burgers for the plane ride.

More than 16 hours and three planes later, Isaac landed in Colombia, in a city called Antigua.

When he reached the baggage claim area, and saw a middle-aged man holding a sign with his name on it, he did not wait or make any assumptions.

"Hi, are you Doctor Ricardo Medina?"

"No, but I will take you to him," the driver said, and led Isaac to a small, red, beat-up car. It was evening and starting to get dark, and the drive took a little under an hour. Isaac saw in the shadows a great deal of foliage lining the roads, which became even thicker when the driver turned down a narrow path leading to a small villa in the forest.

He climbed out of the car and thought it looked more like a jungle than a forest. The driver spoke in broken English: "The doctor knows you will be waiting. There is food in the kitchen. Please help yourself. He will be back in a couple of days."

Isaac uneasily watched the brake lights fade into the darkness, and then let himself into the small house, which held sparse, but well-kept, furniture. He found some food to snack on, and then what looked like a spare bedroom, and slept for 12 hours.

The next morning, he made breakfast and then walked outside. In the light, he confirmed his instincts from the night before—huge trees but interlaced with vines and thick elephant ears and tropical plants he did not recognize. It was beautiful, and he wondered what it looked like from above. The strange sounds in the night heightened his senses. He took a deep breath, filling his lungs with the new, unfamiliar air.

On the second night, the doctor still had not arrived, and he realized that he did not have a phone out there, or even a local number to call. Just the doctor's name and an address on a piece of paper. Not a great plan. His imagination and anxiety began to get the better of him, and then an underlying sense of fear turned into that old familiar anger. By the third afternoon, he was livid at the lack of contact and information. He was pacing the floor, thinking about what he would do if the doctor did not show up soon. Just then, he heard a motor outside, and finally, a very muddy jeep pulled into the front yard area.

He tried to maintain his composure, and walked outside. He saw that it was just one man, already busying himself at the back of the vehicle. Isaac walked up and noticed the strong posture, the wide-brimmed hat, and gray beard. Isaac recognized him from Hugo's picture and guessed the man was in his sixties, yet in better shape than he was!

The man looked over. "Hola! You must be Mac's grandson, Isaac. Yes?"

"That's right. Are you Dr. Medina?"

Extending his hand and smiling broadly, he said, "Yes, but please, call me Ricardo. I do apologize for making you wait, but the jeep broke down about 70 miles from here and it took me until just this morning to get the part and get it moving again."

As Ricardo spoke, he leaned into the back of the jeep and moved around petri dishes, little plastic vials, medical journals, and other equipment between several plastic bins full of medical supplies. Isaac was quickly disarmed by the man's voice, his heartfelt apology, and his sense of purpose in his movements.

"Can you please grab that bin and help me get this stuff in the house?"

Isaac was happy to help, and to actually have something to do.

The two men sat down for a simple dinner of rice and beans, when the doctor began to explain, "I have been here for six years now, working with the local villagers and with the Peace Corps to provide medical assessments. We're seeing a high mortality rate. It's not malaria, but I think it's a distant cousin."

He looked up at Isaac, who was still trying to figure out his role in all this.

The doctor cleared his throat. "In fact, we'll be heading back into the jungle tomorrow."

"Tomorrow?" Isaac repeated, worried. "Don't I need shots or something before we go?"

"Don't worry, our immune systems are more advanced than theirs, and this sickness only affects the villagers in a specific region. Please be ready by 6 a.m. I left a bag that will help keep your clothes dry in the humidity. Pack light—and don't forget the bug spray and first aid kit I left for you. We'll load up the truck with fresh water from the spring in the morning."

The doctor drove fast through the narrow roads, and although the sun was rising, it seemed to be getting darker. Isaac asked the doctor about it.

"Yes, we're heading deeper into the jungle. Triple Canopy. The light plays tricks on you."

They didn't talk much for the next two hours, because the motor was loud and the rocks and mud hitting the bottom of the jeep was even louder at times.

Isaac looked over in surprise when the doctor finally slowed near the end of a broad flowing river. Three men awaited them with three small wooden boats.

"It's the only way to access the villages," the doctor said, "We usually only have one boat for supplies, but we're bringing extra on this trip."

Following Ricardo's lead, Isaac jumped out of the jeep and helped to transfer their gear into the boats, and then climbed in one. The doctor took the lead, and Isaac just stared in awe as they lazily drifted down the slow-moving river, usually staying near the sides. The shoreline was alive with shadowy movement and sounds. Isaac felt as though he was being watched, but did not know by whom or what.

By the time another hour had passed, Isaac began to see signs of human life. Rudimentary huts right near the edge of the river, fishing lines and nets hanging above the water. Villagers wearing scant clothing as they walked the river with long sticks, or moved into the jungle on paths with baskets balanced on their heads.

He saw a man walk up to the end of a makeshift dock, where he stopped at a hole in the wood and began to squat down.

Is that what I think it is? Isaac wondered to himself. He began to smell the stench.

The two boats were side by side, as Isaac and the doctor had been chatting about their priorities once they reached the village.

The doctor understood, and said, "Yes, we are trying to teach them to dig holes and bury their waste, but the jungle floor is soft, and they prefer to just let the river wash away that type of thing."

"Yes, but, what about the people down river?"

"Exactly."

Just as Isaac had anticipated, they rounded a few more bends in the river, and encountered more and more huts and people. Children were splashing and playing in the water. An elderly woman was knee deep in the water, washing strips of cloth, no doubt to be used as clothing.

They finally came to a large turn in the river, and it looked like the hub of activity. The doctor handed Isaac a digital camera and journal. "The village spreads into the jungle around this area, but this is the heart of it," Ricardo explained. "There are about 75 adults and 140 children, and 85% of them are sick.

"Remember, I want you to simply photograph and write down what you see. Document what you observe. We need to understand why this is happening and how we can help them fix it."

It was obvious that the villagers knew the doctor, and trusted him. They looked at Isaac with kindness—but also with caution. The children followed Isaac everywhere.

Once he got up close and followed the doctor into just the first couple of huts, he was shocked by the open wounds and sores, and the way the humidity seemed to increase the foul smell and help breed infection.

He tried to keep up, and to stay out of the way, writing down the date and copying down the patients' names as the doctor spelled them out for him. The doctor also coached him on what to document with photographs, and kept repeating, "We have lots of film, so document what you think might be important."

Pushing past his initial queasiness, Isaac felt like a humanitarian, or philanthropist, for the first time in his life. The doctor told him that the Peace Corps also worked in this area. He wrote down everything the doctor asked, and filled up the camera's hard drive with images of lanced boils, lacerations, and other symptoms. Isaac photographed the open drainage in the middle of the streets that seemed to collect everything, including waste from the huts. He also captured how it drained into the river.

From time to time, he put his gear down and helped the doctor wash his hands.

The doctor was trying to be professional and create a sterile environment, but when he pulled off an old bandage and removed the leaves that had been used to cover the wound, Isaac saw and smelled the effects of gangrene on a child's foot. He felt the doctor's compassion, along with his tangible frustration when he had to replace some bandages with used bandages that had been washed in the river, and then boiled.

At the end of the first day, Isaac was completely exhausted. He shared a hut with the doctor, but could hardly sleep. He found all the new sights and sounds and smells quite overwhelming, and quite sad. As the week ended, they trekked back by boat and then in the jeep to the doctor's villa to resupply. Isaac quietly reflected on all that had just happened.

As the jeep came to a stop in front of the villa, Isaac and the doctor began to unload the jeep. Isaac finally asked what had been gnawing at him. "How can they not see that what they are doing is making them sick?"

"It's the only way they know how," Ricardo responded patiently. "It is their reality. Their whole lives, they have grown up in this environment, and in many ways, their thinking has been shaped by what has been going on for generations. The reality that you and I come from makes things very obvious, so we have to remember that we are dealing with cultural issues as well as generational issues. That is why our work is so important. The evidence that we collect will help us know how to teach and show us how to create change."

They were only in for one night, and shared another meal in the doctor's small kitchen. Always immersed in his work, the doctor ate with one hand and leafed through the journal with the other. He then looked through some of the photographs on the camera's little screen.

He furrowed his brow and asked, "Where is the rest of it?"

"What do you mean?" Isaac asked, confused.

"Why are all the photos like this?"

"I'm sorry, I don't understand," Isaac replied honestly. "You asked me to take pictures of what was going wrong."

"No, I asked you to document what you see. It is interesting, the photographs that you took, and what it says about your focus. And I guess that's where my question is … why are these all photos of wounds and sickness? It's like these are all worst-case scenarios."

Feeling a bit under-appreciated, Isaac snapped back, "Well, isn't a village with 85% sick people a worst-case scenario?"

At that moment, the doctor paused, took a long breath, and then exhaled. He looked around as if he had not done so in a long time, settling in, getting his internal bearings.

"I apologize, my friend, but let me explain what I mean…

"Yes, this is a bad situation for them, but it's all relative. They are simply living their lives the best way they know how. I can understand how jarring it must have been for you, and I really threw you to the wolves. But Mac said you could handle anything I throw at you."

"He did?" Isaac was a bit shocked.

The doctor went on, "I remember feeling the same way, but that was more than five years ago. Now I know those people, so I can look past the surface level. Do me a favor—when we get back tomorrow, just take a step back and ask yourself if you are really capturing an objective view of everything going on, not just the 'bad stuff,' the sickness, okay? I want you to gather evidence of their reality, not just their struggles. This will help my research and the program very much."

Isaac thought for a moment. "Okay. I will try."

"Thank you, Isaac"—and with that, the doctor excused himself for the night.

The next morning, the pair made the trip back to the village, in a single boat this time, and Isaac kept the doctor's advice in mind.

Staring intently ahead, not speaking, taking in his surroundings, Isaac heard a universally delightful sound—children laughing! The boats rounded a bend, and sure enough, a young boy and girl from the village were splashing each other in the river smiling, screeching with joy, as Isaac snapped his first picture.

When they arrived, he followed Ricardo along the muddy paths and back to the huts that he knew held the sickest villagers. Right outside of the "worst" tent, he noticed two men and three women sitting around a pot of boiling water. They were boiling bandages, but they were also all smiling. Smiling! Was there no smiling or laughing the entire week before, or had Isaac literally not even noticed?

That day, and the next several afterward, Isaac dug into his work and documented all that he saw, both healthy and unhealthy. Rather than a medical assistant or record keeper, he felt more like a photojournalist trying to capture the real story on the ground. As he captured more images of people smiling or playing or caring for each other in those harsh conditions, he began to see the villagers as much more free and content than he had at first.

Lying on his cot one night, he realized that his focus had definitely been much too narrow before. The doctor had not limited his field of perspective in any way, but still, Isaac had focused on the worst parts of the experience—almost by default!

A special ritual was approaching, and Isaac was fascinated to see the villagers' excitement about the event. He almost wished they weren't leaving so soon, and then, to his pleasant surprise, the boat broke down. They were stranded for a few days, and the villagers invited him and the doctor to attend the ritual dance and feast.

The sun went down dark in the jungle, but a big moon rose and reflected off the river. A huge bonfire also reflected off the water. Just as he had seen in movies, only more colorful and loud, the entire village gathered in a large circle to watch the festivities. There were lines of children holding long snakes made out of vine, and women dancing with feathered headdresses. The fire made everything glow, and the music was hypnotic.

There were men with spears and booming voices pounding their feet in the dirt and playing drums of animal skin. Children danced and ran all around them, and at one point, they pulled Isaac up to dance, along with Ricardo. As Isaac reveled in the pure fun and joy of the moment, free of his inner dialog for a while, he wondered where all of this colorful garb had come from. He hadn't noticed anything like it in any of the huts, no more than he had noticed how connected and happy the villagers seemed overall, despite their apparent struggles. He smiled along with everyone else, and nodded at every set of eyes he met, but inside he was thinking of

Mac and Hugo and Vick. They knew all along what he was only just now realizing for himself—that he had been walking around with blinders on.

The night culminated in the village with a mother telling a long tale. Isaac did not understand the words, but he did understand that every man, woman, and child was rapt with attention, hanging on to every word and filled with a sense of wonder and pride.

He slept deeply, and dreamed of Amy.

Back at the villa a few days later, the doctor once again reviewed Isaac's notes and photos.

Nodding his head, he said, "Yes, thank you, Isaac. I can see that this is a much more balanced perspective. I hope that helped you to see how we let our minds and personal filters color the world.

"I've found that as a doctor, I have to maintain a sense of objectivity, even when performing a complicated medical procedure. If I don't maintain that sense of observation, I can easily get lost in the sadness of my work, seeing so many people sick and suffering. When I lose my objectivity, I can't find meaningful solutions, and I see my own experiences as a metaphor for life. Most people lose perspective, and ignore all the evidence they have right in front of them about what is possible, and how we can transcend much of our suffering simply by choosing a different perspective."

He paused to take a drink, and then went on, "Some people gather only positive and negative evidence. They live in a world that is very black and white, their way or the highway, you know?"

Isaac nodded. "Yeah, I see what you mean."

"But another way to live is to look at the results and the evidence. Instead of right and wrong, how about asking what is working and what is not working? How about looking for evidence of what is possible and what one has accomplished, instead of evidence of our own limitations?"

"I agree, but still, you live in a very unique environment out here," Isaac pointed out. "I'm not sure it's so simple back in the real world."

"Isn't it, though?" asked the doctor. Isaac paused and thought.

"Well, food for thought, my friend," Ricardo smiled. "I cannot thank you enough for your friendship and support these past few weeks. I am heading back out tomorrow, but you will not be joining me. May I see the key?"

He had been expecting this, and when the doctor paused to look at the key, Isaac had already guessed which part belonged to him—the little knob from an old microscope.

The doctor led Isaac into a side room and opened a small safe under his desk. He pulled out a small object and handed it to Isaac. It was a wooden box with brass hinges and a brass latch, and appeared to be very old. As Isaac opened it up, he found a small black-handled magnifying glass.

The doctor could see the question in Isaac's eyes. "It was given to me by my father when I graduated medical school. I was going to pass it on to my son when I had my own family, but I have been so busy with my career and taking care of other people that I never took the time to have a family of my own. You are the closest I have as a son, because I look at Mac as my brother. So, I am passing this on to you, and hope you will pass it on when it's time."

Next, he handed Isaac a piece of paper that said, "Chad Rupp. St. George,

Utah" and included a phone number. Apparently, Isaac was headed to the southwestern United States. As always, he waited until the plane ride to read the note he had found the next morning:

Dear Isaac,

Results reveal opportunities.

Opinions reveal peoples' realities.

-Dr. Ricardo Medina

Faith and Hope

The flight from Chicago to a short layover in Denver was uneventful. Isaac then jumped on a smaller plane that took him to southern Utah. It was mid-morning in May, and the landscape below him was utterly gorgeous. Deep canyons and rocky cliffs, all turning a darker red as they approached their destination.

Looking out of his window just above the wing, his eyes grew wide. The small craft was heading toward a mountain ridge, which seemed to be the runway. The closer they got, the more he noticed the strong crosswind jostling the plane left and right. He hadn't noticed how much he was grinding his teeth until they were safely on the ground and he heard that old familiar sound of air brakes.

There was no airport terminal; he simply walked down some metal steps and was directed into the airport's small building. Right away, he spotted a man walking toward him, openly excited and instantly friendly. Isaac immediately noticed that the man was deeply tanned, with muscular arms and calves.

He held out his hand, "Hi, I'm Chad. You must be Isaac."

"That's me."

"Cool, man, let's grab your bags and head out. We need to be somewhere in about an hour."

Chad was about six feet tall, and his brown hair was speckled with grey. He drove a silver Toyota 4-Runner that was covered with red dust and dirt. He talked most of the 20 minutes, giving Isaac a brief history: seasoned mountain climber, expedition guide, self-proclaimed desert rat. Ran his own climbing business, in which he contracted with local resorts and taught tourists about climbing and surviving in the desert. His arms were wiry and muscular, and his hands were calloused on the steering wheel—no doubt from climbing this incredible terrain.

"You ever climb?" Chad finally asked.

"Nope," Isaac replied, "but that's about to change, isn't it?"

"Well, not today, but yes, that's all about to change. I'll do my best to show you what I think Mac wants me to show you, and you'll be totally safe, okay? No worries.

"Did you know that if you'd draw a hundred-mile-wide circle with St. George at the center, you'd find the highest concentration of national parks on the continent? Pretty cool, huh?"

Isaac noticed that Chad tapped his fingers, laughed out loud, asked questions, and talked a lot, seemingly to fill up any quiet space. Isaac liked him, and admired his high energy and genuine sense of hospitality.

They pulled up to a small house with two pickups, several cars, and an SUV parked at random angles in the front. Chad hopped out, grabbed Isaac's bags from the back, and led him into the house.

They walked past a large open closet full of backpacks, ropes, and other climbing gear. They passed another room and Isaac noticed a collage of photos, no doubt Chad's climbing expeditions. Next to those was a large map with many pins all over Utah and surrounding states, and a couple up in Montana.

The hallway opened up to a living room, where a group was gathered together watching TV. There was a kayak in the corner. Chad didn't even slow down, declaring, "Everybody, this is Isaac. Isaac, meet the gang."

Almost in unison, almost as though rehearsed, they greeted him with a "Hi, Isaac!" Isaac wondered if they might regularly have guests moving through. Chad finally stopped in a small room, dropped Isaac's bags near a single mattress on the floor, and said, "This is where you'll crash, okay? Bathroom's up the hall, second door on the left.

"Oh, by the way, that was my son and his girlfriend, and a few of their friends. He's 26, spent a couple of years in the Army, but he's been living back at home with me for a while this year."

Chad looked around, looked at Isaac, smiled distractedly as if he was making some calculation in his head, and then looked at his watch.

"Okay, we gotta roll."

Chad explained on the way that they were driving to a place called Green Valley Resort to pick up a group in a van and take them out for some climbing lessons; Isaac would be his assistant.

When they arrived, Chad pointed to a large van across the parking lot and said, "That's our ride. It should be unlocked. Can you move the gear from my truck into the back of that one? I'll be right back." He then walked into a door marked "Guest Center."

Just as Isaac finished moving the gear, Chad walked out leading a group of about 10 guests, most of them appearing to be in their fifties and sixties. Chad's boundless energy and quick talk became the epitome of charm and customer service.

He introduced Isaac as his helper, and then asked the small group of guests to load into the van. He joked and engaged them in conversation the whole drive, and within 10 minutes, they were parking near a trailhead called Chuckawalla. Isaac was excited to walk into the Mars-looking rock formations he had noticed from the plane.

Isaac laughed along with everyone else at Chad's non-stop humor. He also couldn't help but notice that several of the guests seemed to act very entitled.

"Will this take long?" one of them asked impatiently, and then his wife shushed him and whispered, "Don't be rude!"

Chad asked if anyone needed to use the washroom, as several people were talking in the rear of the group. He then explained that they were going to walk a couple of hundred feet down the trail, and pointed and led the way.

Halfway down, one of the women who hadn't been listening began to ask about the bathroom. She got an exasperated look from another guest, but Chad didn't hesitate. "Okay, it's right back up there near the truck. Buddy teams only."

She looked at her husband, and the two walked back up the trail together.

Isaac then watched as Chad set up shop near a large, flat rock. He invited everyone to find a rock and have a seat, and then he climbed on top of the rock as if on a small stage. He covered some safety issues, and explained how everyone would get a chance to wear the harness and do a short climb. Isaac was clumsy, but for the most part, provided Chad with the equipment he needed, both during the demonstration, and then during the actual climbs.

Walking back up the trail an hour and a half later, he explained, "If anyone wants to do the level 2 group, the next one's on Friday and it will include some larger climbs. There are four levels, so if you're in town for a while I hope to see you again."

Chad was efficient, and before long, he and Isaac had dropped off the group, transferred the equipment back into the 4-Runner, and were headed home for the night.

"That was really interesting," Isaac told Chad. "But how do you put up with those bratty guests?"

"Oh, they're not so bad," Chad chuckled. "I think most people put on a good front, like they're doing okay inside, but I've learned to give them space and look deeper. I know they're not angry at me; it's not personal—it's the stuff going on in their own lives."

Twice a day for the next four days, Isaac felt more and more like a packing mule roasting in the hot sun. It was hard work, and Isaac wasn't allowed to climb with the guests. (Liability issues with the resort.)

Finally, it was his turn to climb. On Sunday, Chad drove Isaac to a nearby town called Springdale, known as the gateway to Zion National Park. The only way Chad could describe the craggy peaks and multi-colored vistas was something out of Lord of the Rings, or Jurassic Park. Just unbelievable scale and scope. Breathtaking, really.

Isaac seemed lost in the moment, his mouth hanging open a bit as he craned his neck to see the massive walls of rock that appeared around every new bend. As Isaac tried his best to listen, Chad gave Isaac a pretty detailed history lesson on the park, and how the tunnel was built through the side of a huge rock mountain. Chad pulled over within sight of an 80-foot rock tower as wide as four trucks. He explained that this massive piece of stone had fallen to its current position hundreds of thousands of years ago.

"And this is where we're climbing?" Isaac asked, a bit worried, craning his neck to look up at the overwhelming height.

"Yes, but not all the way up. Not yet, at least." Chad wasn't joking.

Isaac had watched a dozen or so groups put on harnesses and do basic short climbs, so he geared up as Chad explained how they would climb up to the first ledge together, and then he would have to find his way for about 30 feet until Chad could see him again.

"We'll be able to talk, but I just won't have visibility on that one section," Chad pointed. He went on, "Remember, I've got you all tied in, so even if you fall, you're not really going to fall. You're going to drop no more than five feet and then swing around a bit. But you won't fall, okay?"

With their helmets and gear, they both did a slow ascent to the ledge Chad had mentioned. Isaac felt pretty good, and was able to either find strong handholds or just hunch over and climb over the large rocks leading up.

Chad then explained that he would go first, and showed Isaac exactly where to grab hold, as well as the route of the climb around a large rock.

"You got this. I'll see you up there."

Chad then climbed up, yelling out instructions the whole way, and then safely guided Isaac using verbal commands until they met up on another, higher ledge. Chad said, "Great job, man. You're a natural. See, totally safe when you have the right equipment and the right attitude. Let's chill here for a bit."

Chad sat down on the ledge, and Isaac followed. As Chad pulled out water and granola bars, Isaac finally took his eye from the rock and lifted his gaze. "Beautiful," he whispered when he saw the view. The road had climbed up and up, but Isaac had not been able to see behind him in the truck. Then, as they had walked up a short but steep trail to reach the base of the tower, Isaac had been too nervous and focused to notice the view, but their current position offered the most amazing vista Isaac had ever seen. It was difficult for his eyes to take it all in, and the depth perception almost gave him vertigo. He shook his head and took a sip of water "This is really something else, Chad!" he said, impressed. "I don't know about climbing to the top of this thing, though!"

When Chad did not reply with some funny quip or remark, Isaac looked over. Chad was gazing out at the same view with the curiosity and love of a child. He was quiet, at peace, not talking for perhaps the first time since Isaac had met him.

After about 10 minutes of eating and staring, he started talking again, pointing out two red-tailed hawks soaring past nearby, but more slowly and in a hushed tone, as if they were in a library or a church.

"Here's the thing, Isaac," Chad said next. "Faith is the first step. My son was a paratrooper in the Army and they pounded this idea into his head: trust your equipment. In other words, once you've done all the safety checks and you know the chute is packed properly, don't think about it anymore. Just jump!

"It's the same thing here. I have great faith in the systems I use for climbing, in the equipment. Yes, accidents happen. Yes, I will sometimes feel fear. But I can minimize and push past those things with the best equipment and best attitude."

"You keep saying that, about the 'best attitude.' What do you mean?" Isaac asked.

"I'm still talking about faith, or hope, or whatever you want to call it. As soon as I give faith some power, some energy, I can take one more step, move one more foot or inch. And then the faith snowballs, and my confidence increases, and I can see new possibilities."

Isaac was eating his own granola bar, still astounded by the view around him, listening very closely to Chad. He knew this was some good wisdom, and he wanted to learn.

"When we can add a sense of value to our fear, such as the desire to push through to that next peak, that next goal in life, then we can challenge the fear," Chad continued. "And when we come out on the other side of fear, we feel more hope, and we can create a vision of how we want things to be."

Chad pulled an extra cord of rope from his backpack. "I like to use rope as an analogy. When you step on the rope over and over during your climbs, it presses these tiny particles of glass/sandstone into the fibers. Over time, the sand starts to dig in at the micro level and deteriorate the rope's tinsel strength.

"For us, when we let negative self-talk come in, those words and images in our minds start to break down the overall structure from within and hinder our ability to create hope."

"I've never thought of it that way before," Isaac mused.

"What's wrong with this rope?" Chad asked, handing it to Isaac.

"Looks fine, right? But when I run it between my fingers like this, I can feel little voids on the inside of the sheath. On the outside, everything looks fine, but on the inside, the rope has been compromised. One small spot within a 200-foot rope can kill you. The loss of hope can be devastating, leading to depression and keeping us from moving forward in our lives."

Over the next few weeks, Isaac continued to help Chad with his climbing classes, and enjoyed having dinner in the local restaurants. He was surprised at how quickly his confidence increased in climbing, and gave full credit to Chad's outstanding guidance and support.

He sensed that Chad was getting him ready for his biggest challenge yet, and was not surprised when they planned another trip to Zion National Park. Once again, they drove up to the massive spire, and Isaac felt his heart beating, his mind getting the best of him. But he reminded himself that not once did Chad leave him in an unsafe spot. He had felt completely safe on every climb, and he was confident all of Chad's guests would say the same thing.

Walking up to the base of the tower, he tried to muster all his faith: in Chad, in the gear, in himself, and in what he had learned these past weeks. The climb was difficult, and physically demanding on his whole body, and at one point, his left fingers went a little numb after he held on in a specific spot for 10 minutes, looking for his next move.

About halfway up the largest section he had ever attempted to traverse, Isaac lost it. He didn't know where to go, and didn't dare look down. Faith be damned. He wanted down. Now.

"Chad, I'm stuck man. I'm stuck right here," Isaac yelled. "Can you guide me which way to go?"

"Up, Isaac. Up!" Chad yelled back. "Always up!"

Muttering under his breath, Isaac focused and found a foothold, and then the rest of the climb eventually became easier. Twenty minutes later, they were perched on top of the 80-foot tower, and the view was even more remarkable. The rock walls of the canyon still extended another 300 feet above them.

Chad turned to Isaac after a bit. "So, how did faith help you make this climb?"

Isaac paused. "Well, at first I had to have faith in you, and then the equipment. Then faith in how you taught me where to place my hands and feet. I had to have faith in what you were telling me and I had to learn to have faith in the rock. But once I got out of view and was on my own, I had to quiet my negative self-talk and reach up and look for the next handhold, hoping it was there. When I found that handhold, it gave me more hope and faith in myself."

That same evening, Isaac was helping to clean up the dishes after dinner, and Chad said, "Dude, it's time. Follow me."

He led Isaac into his relaxation room. There was a small desk with a large book about the Colorado Plateau, and another one about local hikes. Chad moved a box and revealed a small door. He asked Isaac for the key, and then looked at it, focusing on a piece of climbing equipment that Isaac now knew was a camming device.

He opened the door with the key, then reached in and pulled out a length of paracord looped into a necklace, hanging from it was a small hexagon-shaped piece of metal. Chad explained that it was a small anchoring device used to push into cracks to help secure the climber.

"Now you are ready for the next part of your journey," he said. "We are sending you to Wyoming. To a small town called Sheridan. Our buddy Charlie will be waiting."

The next morning, Chad was gone before Isaac woke up, and Chad's son drove him to the bus station. Aside from some friendly small talk, the ride was quiet. After they shook hands and Isaac climbed out of the truck, the young man honked the horn and rolled down the window. "Here, I almost forgot." He handed Isaac an envelope with his name on it.

Isaac checked in, and then sat down to wait for boarding and read the note:

Dear Isaac,

I was blown away by the growth I saw in you. Mac was right. You are meant for this journey that you are on. I remember when you were a small boy, and Mac telling me that he knew that you would be the one.

Remember, let your faith and hope anchor you, and when you get scared of moving your feet, remember, up, up — always up!

-Chad

Movement

The bus ride from Utah to Sheridan, Wyoming, took about 12 hours. Isaac had not slept, and he was feeling grumpy. With the romance of the desert behind him, he somehow felt that this next adventure was going to be even more difficult. Why exactly am I doing this? He wondered. Oh yeah, to become a better person, blah blah blah…

Isaac walked around the bus station, looking for a sign, looking for someone. When he had checked the whole station, he walked out of the front door. An arm stuck out of a white Ford pickup and waved him over, then honked the horn.

Isaac moved closer and peered into the window.

An older-looking cowboy smiled. "You Mac's boy?"

Isaac nodded, but before he could say something, the cowboy said, "I'm Charlie. Hop in."

Wow, curbside service.

Charlie drove up the busy main street, then made a sharp U-turn right in front of a big truck with a horse trailer. Isaac braced himself, but Charlie moved out of the way just in time. He then sped down three more blocks, and pulled up in front of a J. C. Penney.

Without a word, he climbed out of the truck and walked in. Isaac wasn't sure if he was supposed to follow, but after a moment, the door opened back up and Charlie waved him in impatiently. Isaac went inside the store.

Charlie grabbed a couple of pairs of jeans, a pack of T-shirts, a button-down western-style shirt, and tube socks, and then handed them all to Isaac.

"What size shoe do you wear? How about hat size?" he asked.

Isaac was a bit taken aback. "Um, size 10, and I'm not sure about the hat."

Handing him a pair of brown cowboy boots, Charlie plopped a hat on Isaac's head, which promptly fell over his ears. He pulled the hat off and replaced it with another, as if dressing a mannequin.

"Yup. That'll do it," he said, and then walked up to the register.
Both men stood in silence as the woman behind the register scanned all the tags. "That'll be $140."

Isaac waited. But Charlie looked over at him and said, "Well, pay the lady," and walked out the store.

Another quiet drive. Hank Williams on the radio. The closer they got to the ranch, the bumpier the road. But the place was so green and lush, it reminded Isaac of a postcard.

Charlie walked Isaac into the main house, and introduced him to his wife, Tammy. She gave him a big hug and said, "Well, you look like your grandpa, and believe me, that's a compliment. He's one good-lookin' man!"

Isaac laughed. "Thank you!"

"So, let me guess," Tammy said warmly. "Charlie over there hasn't said more than three words since he picked you up, right?" Isaac looked over at Charlie, who offered a knowing smile.

"I find this all so exciting!" exclaimed Tammy. "Where have you all been now?"

"So far, to Montana, Chicago, Italy, South America, and Utah, and now here, ma'am," Isaac replied.

"And are you enjoying yourself?"

Charlie was watching closely, as he filled a glass of water from the sink.

"Most of the time, yes. It's been quite the adventure so far."

"How is your grandpa? Oh, and how is Hugo? We haven't seen him since we took a trip to Italy about eight years ago."

Charlie sat down and listened as Isaac responded to Tammy, and seemed to soften around the edges just a bit.

Tammy asked about Chad, and Charlie broke in, "Yeah, how is that old mountain goat? He tried getting me up with his gadgets on his rocks and I told him he was crazy. Who would climb up a rock, just to come right back down?"

So the man can talk, after all, Isaac thought. Just a little slow to warm up.

After a quick dinner, Charlie grabbed a blanket and sheets and walked Isaac out to the bunkhouse, which looked like a barn from the outside. He introduced him to two young men playing a game of cards on their bunks, said, "See you at 5:30 sharp," and then shut the door.

Isaac asked where he could find an empty bunk, and fell asleep quickly, still in his clothes. One of the other ranch hands nudged him at 5 in the morning and said, "Time to go get it."

Isaac soon realized that Charlie was the taskmaster. This was his ranch, and he wanted things done a certain way. Almost right away, Isaac was assigned to a team branding cattle. Aside from spending time on Mac's property, Isaac had never worked on a farm. He had no idea what he was doing, and no one was explaining. So he just watched and stayed out of the way.

Another ranch hand sensed his reluctance. "Come on," he said, led him over to a group of men standing near a corral. Within minutes, five more men on horses came from the tree line, leading about 50 head of cattle into the corral. The men on horses were yelling and whooping, and the men on the ground began to fan out and herd the cattle into the opened gates. Isaac followed his informal mentor and helped as best he could, although he was unsure about getting too close to the wild-eyed animals.

And then it was time for branding. Isaac watched as the men grabbed a single calf and pulled it out from the group. It began wailing loudly, along with another larger animal, probably its mother.

The men moved the young animal a few yards away from the corral, where another was heating up some branding irons. One of the men swiftly stepped in and grabbed the calf on one side and reached his left arm around the calf's neck while his right hand grabbed his rear flank. He then lifted the animal up in the air, and dropped it violently on the ground. The calf seemed to lose all the air in its lungs, and its eyes showed pure fear and panic. Isaac involuntarily took a step back. What bizarre world had he stumbled into?

The wailing only increased as the first man was joined by a second, who quickly immobilized the calf. Next, the brander came in and placed the hot brand on the animal's flank. More screams, and the smell of burning hair and flesh. Everyone seemed unfazed by the screaming, but Isaac was trying not to seem completely horrified.

Another worker stepped in and applied a shot of antibiotics, while another cut a small chunk out of the animal's ear. Yet another placed glue in the tip of the horn nubs, which would prevent the horns from growing. When they finally released the calf, it promptly ran back to its momma. Isaac didn't know who was more traumatized—him or the calf.

The work was hard, and took all of Isaac's energy for him to keep up. The days quickly bled into weeks, with the never-ending cycle of work, eat, wash, sleep, and repeat. Isaac was tired and growing more annoyed by the day. Charlie stopped by his bunk one Sunday. "You know a thing or two about horses, right?"

"Sure, I grew up around horses."

"That's good, because I've got a project for you," Charlie said, and walked Isaac over to the horse barn.

They approached a dark-brown horse with glistening eyes and large yellow teeth mashing on some hay. "This is Biscuit," Charlie introduced. "I'd like you to take care of her. But I have to tell you that she was abused by a previous owner, so go easy, okay?"

Isaac started right away, using his limited skills to lead Biscuit out into the pasture a bit so he could have a look. The horse was hard to work with, and didn't trust him yet. Still, Isaac was determined to do his part, and fulfill whatever Charlie had in store for both him and the horse. He kept working with the horse, feeding it, brushing it out, and riding it each day. Isaac began to realize that Biscuit wasn't going to make this easy for him, so he decided to back up and start with the basics.

He started with the halter and a lead rope, and began walking around the ranch, the corrals, and the round pen. He just spent time with her and established a basic relationship of trust. Next, he reintroduced the bitten saddle, but he didn't ride her. He just led her and continued to feed and brush her, creating a safe space.

Finally, when he felt the time was right, Isaac decided to ride and work with her in the round pen one day. Mac had shown him before how to assert himself and create trust in a pen like this. He had said the round pen allows a rider to work on reining by riding in circles and reining it the same time, then reversing direction and reining to follow suit.

Halfway through the exercise, something spooked Biscuit, and she froze up, pinned her ears back, and backed up. It was as if she had found a corner in a round pen. She took a deep breath, so deep that Isaac felt as though she was going to split him in half, and held it. She was quivering, and Isaac knew she was about to start bucking.

Mac had taught him to never climb off a horse when it is going to buck. On the contrary, Mac had told him to grab a tuft of mane in one hand then grab the horn and the reins with the other hand, and to kick his heels down and toes out and "hang on for the ride of his life."

But just then, a little voice told him, "Get off the horse." Then softly again, "Isaac, get off the horse."

After a third time, he slinked off the saddle and stood quietly beside the horse. Biscuit was still quivering with fear all over, her legs locked in place. He knew that if she kicked or started bucking, he could be in big trouble. But again, he felt compelled to do something completely out of the ordinary.

With the reins still in his hand, he gently put his shoulder to her shoulder and leaned in. She moved ever so slightly, but rocked back to her original position. He pushed again, this time a little harder, and Biscuit took two short steps forward, and exhaled loudly. Her ears came up and her tail began to swish.

Isaac climbed back on and got back to work. After a few minutes of riding in circles and pondering what had just happened, Isaac began to feel philosophical in the September afternoon air. He thought about all the times he had been frozen with fear, unable to move, feeling backed into a corner with his defenses up, not sure whether to shut down or lash out—quivering and panicking, just like Biscuit had done.

That night at dinner, it was quiet, until Charlie said, "I saw you working with Biscuit today. That was a risky move, but impressive all the same."

"Oh, you saw that?" Isaac perked up. "Yeah, it was a pretty surreal moment. Not sure why I felt the need to push her through it. Mac always taught me to hold on for dear life."

"What did she do?" Tammy wondered.

"Biscuit was bowed up, pinned ears, ready to go to buckin', but this one here," Charlie chuckled, motioning toward Isaac, "got her moving again. I have never seen anything like it. He just climbed down, cool as a summer breeze, shouldered up to her, just leaning in. That old girl took two steps forward as if life just started over again."

Charlie looked Isaac straight in the eyes, and said, "You know, son, horses have a sense about them; they tend to know the lessons we need the most in our lives, and they have a peculiar way of teaching them to us."

Charlie cocked his head to the side, smiled, then said, "I bet you thought that you were teaching her."

After Charlie excused himself, Isaac thanked Tammy for a wonderful meal and headed back to his bunk, reflecting on his journey for the past few months. He knew that putting himself in treatment created motion. And then going up to Montana and having a breakdown in the middle of the woods needed to happen. He could see it clearly now. Once he asked for help, Mac seemed to open a new reservoir in his heart. He seemed more willing to help, and sent him on this journey.

Now, more determined than ever, Isaac threw himself into the work and doubled his efforts with Biscuit. After another month, Isaac reported to Charlie that the horse was ready for whatever work he needed her to do.

"I agree," said Charlie. "Now let's go for a ride, son."

"Now?"

"Yes, now."

Isaac turned to another ranch hand and asked, "Hey, can you brush her out for me?" and then followed Charlie to the truck.

They started driving through the city and out into the hills on a winding tree-lined road. They passed a sign that read "Story, Wyoming" and soon pulled up to a log cabin with a big wooden porch.

Isaac followed Charlie inside and into a study, where he approached a small door in the wall. He turned to Isaac and asked for the key. Charlie's section of the key was an old rowel disk off an old spur.

Charlie opened the door and pulled out a pair of old spurs. He handed them to Isaac and said, "I won these in a bucking contest when I was 18. Pretty much wore them out. They remind me of a time when I was struggling and not feeling in control of my life. The next year, I decided to buy a piece of land and a horse and couple of cows and started moving. The rest is history. I'd like you to have them, to remind you to keep your feet moving, too.

"Speaking of your feet moving," Charlie continued, "you're going to California to visit an old beachcomber buddy of mine, Gage."

Charlie handed Isaac a piece of stationary marked "Kings Rope, Sheridan, Wyoming," with an address and phone number. As always, he left early the next morning with little fanfare, and pocketed the note that had been slipped under the door. He waited until they had gained altitude, and the flight attendant brought him a cup of water and a bag of pretzels. As he snacked in comfort, he pulled out the note:

Dear Isaac,

Whatever Biscuit taught you is what you needed. That day you got her moving, I saw a shift in you. Keep moving, even when life bucks you off.

-Charlie

Meditation and Prayer

---•••---

Quick flight to San Diego, California, and then a shuttle to Encinitas. Isaac asked the driver to drop him off at the address Charlie had given him: Gage Redding, 44 West Pacifica Lane. He stepped out onto the sidewalk of a little surf shop. Small tables in the front featured weather-washed shells and various pieces of jewelry. Old surfboards were nailed to the walls. A woman in sandals, a white shirt, and a loose, tie-dyed skirt walked out, looking for something on one of the tables. She caught Isaac's eye and smiled. "Hi, can I help you?"

"Yes, my name's Isaac. Charlie sent me. Or, I guess Mac sent me. But I'm looking for Gage."

"Well, you found us. I'm his wife, Sharon. He'll be right back. Come on in."

"Thank you," Isaac said, and followed her through the hanging beads in the doorway. Inside was a colorful collection of shirts, skirts, shells, surfboards, and all kinds of little tourist mementos seemingly made from nautical objects. A candle and incense were burning behind the counter, where Sharon seated herself. With the light coming in from a side window and lighting up her hair, she looked like a wise angel.

"Gage will be happy to see you," she said warmly. "Oh, there he is now!"

She pointed out to the front door.

Isaac followed her gaze and saw a large man facing the other way, talking to three young men holding surfboards. He was making large gestures with his hands, and the men were doubled over with laughter. Gage seemed to be at least six foot four, and was wearing sandals and an orange swimsuit with no shirt. His blondish-gray hair cascaded down to his shoulders, and his sinewy muscles were deeply tanned by the sun. Isaac continued to watch as Gage hugged each of the men, and then turned to walk into the shop.

"Babe, this is Isaac," Sharon introduced.

Gage turned instantly to Isaac with open arms and said, "Hey, brother! I'm very glad you're here. Bring it in."

After a long hug, Gage went on, "I'm excited to be a little part of your journey, man. Let's make the most of it and get started right away, okay?"

"Sure!" Isaac replied enthusiastically, appreciating the aura of this man. "Yes, of course."

"First, let me show you where you'll be staying."

As Sharon said, "See you later," Gage walked Isaac out the back of the shop to a small house just a few feet away, and then to a back room in that house. It was more of a closet, and the bed was a cot on a small patio overlooking the beach.

"Okay, leave your stuff, change into some shorts, and let's head out," Gage directed.

Gage led Isaac around the back of the house and down some wooden stairs straight to the beach, past a simple sign that said "SURF LESSONS," with half a dozen surfboards under a small canopy. A young woman was sitting nearby, reading a book, headphones in her ears. "Thanks Brooke," Gage said to her. "I'm back. You can take off for the day. Oh, and this is Isaac. He'll be helping us out for a while."

"Nice to meet you, Isaac," Brooke smiled, and then headed up the beach.

Gage seemed about to speak, but then a couple with two young kids walked up. Gage walked out to meet them. "Hi, interested in some surf lessons?"

"Yes," said the woman. "But how old do the kids have to be?"

"That's up to you, but we recommend at least six." Gage knelt down and spoke to the kids, a brother and sister. "How old are you?"

"Seven," answered the little girl.

"Nine," her brother replied.

Gage stood back up and continued talking to the parents, who set up lessons for the following day. As Gage interacted with the family, Isaac swept his gaze up and down the beach. It was a Wednesday, but the beach was quite busy. There were people of all ages, some in the water, some sunbathing, and an intermittent stream of people jogging or walking up and down the shore. And ahead of him, the huge blue mass of the ocean. The smells and sounds of the beach. He could even hear the wind chimes back up at Gage's place.

I could really get used to this, Isaac thought.

The family of four left, and then Gage came back and sat down next to Isaac, but faced him directly. He stared directly into his eyes, and while Isaac saw only kindness there, he looked away after a few seconds that felt too long.

"So, what's your story, Isaac? Tell me what I need to know."

Isaac somehow knew what he meant, and summarized his shady past, the drug addiction, the last year of his life on this journey. He also shared the truth that he wasn't sure what was going to happen in his life next.

"Thanks for sharing all that with me. But how are you doing now?"

"Well, I have a good job waiting for me in Chicago, so I might end up there," Isaac answered, now thinking about Amy. "And Wyoming was hard work, but I had some cool experiences working with this amazing horse."

"No, no, man," Gage laughed. "I mean, how are you doing right NOW?"

"Like, as in right at this moment?"

"Yes, today, right here, right now. How does it feel to be Isaac, sitting on the beach, right now?" Gage clarified, and swept his hand over the beach as if it were his own living room.

Isaac paused, thought about it, looked around, and said, "I guess it feels pretty good. It's just that the more I learn, the more I realize how much I screwed my life up."

"You mean your external life?"

Isaac was confused. "As opposed to what?"

"Your internal life," Gage answered.

"I don't understand," Isaac admitted.

"I'm just saying, that we have this external life, where we spend a lot of time thinking about what people see and think about us," Gage explained. "But then we have an inner, spiritual life. Even if we're not religious, there's no way around it. This is a mystical, unexplainable life we're living. We have a spirit, a chi, some kind of life force that makes us unique, and makes us different from all the other species on the planet. And no one can really explain it—this thing we call human consciousness. Do you agree?"

Isaac shrugged. "I guess so. Doesn't feel so mystical sometimes."

"Maybe your external life is drowning out the internal one. Just think about it, Isaac—that water is sticking to the planet because of gravity, and covering two-thirds of the surface. We surf on it with our little boards, but meanwhile, we're spinning through space at a million miles an hour and our galaxy is only one of billions! There are more than 200 scientific conditions that are perfectly tuned to make life possible. Now you tell me that isn't unexplainable and magical!"

"Well, yeah, when you put it that way—it's pretty hard to comprehend," Isaac replied, smiling, now thinking about Gage's words.

"Well, listen man, I've had my external struggles, too. Childhood abuse, addiction, running from the law, all of it. I've been down so low that I didn't know if I could go on living. Then I was a soldier with Mac and the other guys, you know. And I didn't do so well after the war.

"But these days, here in my sixties, I've never been so free. And it's not because I'm rich. It's because I've connected with my inner life. Look, I'm not going to try to convince you to see the world the way I see it. I'm just going to show you a little piece of it, and you can decide what to take and what to leave."

"Okay, cool, I appreciate that."

Gage then explained to Isaac that he might sometimes watch over the shop, explain how they ran the surf lessons, and how sometimes he would just sit under the canopy and wait for customers. If someone had a question Isaac couldn't answer, or wanted lessons right away, he could call him or Sharon on the little walkie-talkie and they would help.

"We're always somewhere nearby," Gage reassured Isaac. "Basically, I'd say just relax a bit and get a feel for our life here on the edge of the continent. By the way, you ever surf?"

"Sounds good, and no, but I went snowboarding once. Does that count?"

Gage laughed. "Nope."

That night, Isaac shared a simple meal of fish tacos with mango salsa, and then crashed on the hammock to the sound of the waves. At first, the "noise" was overpowering, distracting, but then he drifted off and did not wake for 10 hours.

Still, it was only 7 a.m., and Sharon was in the shop making coffee and opening the windows. "Good morning," she smiled. "How did you sleep?"

"Really well, actually. Thank you."

"Gage is down on the beach. Want some coffee? And would you bring this one to him for me?"

With two mugs in hand, Isaac made his way down the back stairs to the beach. As he approached, he noticed that the canopy was not yet set up. But a hundred yards to the right, he saw Gage sitting cross-legged with a white shirt on, eyes closed and facing the beach. Isaac hesitated, but before long, Gage began to move around and perform stretches.

Isaac walked over. "Good morning. Brought you some coffee."

Gage looked up, took the coffee, and said, "Thanks, Isaac. Good day to you. Join me."

Isaac sat down, and asked, "Do you mind if I ask what you were doing? Were you praying or meditating or something?"

"No, I don't mind at all," Gage smiled. "I was meditating, but praying, too. There is a very fine line between the two, and often they blend together.

"To me, meditation is just connecting and quieting my mind so I can engage more fully with the moments of my life, and my relationships. But that usually leads me to prayer, where I am thanking my higher power for all the abundance around me, and asking for guidance and support."

Gage turned to face Isaac. "You pray?"

"No, not for a long time. I grew up going to church, but it turned me off and I stopped going as soon as I turned 18."

"Yeah, I get that." Gage changed the subject. "You wanna try surfing today before we open up?"

"Sure."

A half-hour later, the two men were standing at the edge of the water, surfboards under their arms and wet suits on. Gage directed Isaac to put his board down in the sand, and then demonstrated how he would go from a lying position on the board to a squatting position, knees bent. Isaac practiced this move a few dozen times, and then they moved the instruction into the shallow water. Isaac slapped at the water and berated himself after falling off the board five times in a row.

Gage patiently gave him pointers, and then said, "I'm gonna go out a bit more and show you what the full motion looks like. You wait here and watch."

Isaac watched as Gage paddled away and then lay on his board and craned his neck to look at the waves coming in, as though he were reading the water. At just the right moment, as a small wave began to crest, Gage stood up and smoothly rode the wave all the way past Isaac to the shore.

Isaac tried this a few times, but soon realized that he needed a lot more practice before he could get up smoothly. For the next several weeks, Isaac got caught up in working the shop or the surf lesson tent, running errands for Sharon, and practicing his surfing. He had decided that he definitely was not a natural at the sport.

One day after work, the sun was setting and the water was a bright gold. Isaac was out alone, trying to catch some small waves. He was sore from doing the same thing the day before, and before long, was slapping at the water and berating himself. He gave up, and headed to shore, frustrated once again.

Gage was there. "You can leave your stuff here. Let's go for a walk."

They walked silently for about half a mile, until Gage found the spot he had perhaps intended. It was a little cove with a few large rocks.

"Sit with me."

Isaac did, and Gage asked, "May I show you some relaxation techniques?"

"Sure."

"Okay, just close your eyes. Listen. The difference between chaos and control is that the chaos is external and the control is internal. The two sides need each other, like light and dark. We keep trying to eliminate chaos, but the more we do that, the more chaos we create. However, when we create control within us, we can live with the world as it is.

"The crashing of the waves we can hear right now—that is chaos. As you paddle out and get past the break, if you try to push over the wave, it will topple you. Even this cove we're sitting in was once made of rock, part of the land mass. Over time, the water even overcame the rocks, and they can last a lot longer than us.

"But if you don't try to control and dominate the wave, and instead just accept and go through it, the wave washes over you. You become one with the wave. And guess what? Life is just like that—a continuous series of waves.

"Now, take a long breath in, and then a long breath out," Gage instructed. Isaac copied him. "Now just focus on the breath, and the sound of the waves. If a thought pops up, just let it fade away. Try not to focus on anything but your breath."

Isaac knew that Gage was only trying to help, but he just felt silly. Meditation wasn't his thing; it was Gage's. He felt distracted and embarrassed as people walked or jogged by them.

Ten minutes later, Gage opened his eyes and said, "How was that?"

"Fine, I guess," Isaac shrugged. "Just not my thing."

"What's not your thing? Clearing your mind and feeling more relaxed?"

"No, that's not what I meant. I just feel stupid sitting here on the beach, not talking or whatever. And then people looking at us."

Gage sighed. "Listen, please don't take offense, but it seems like you are more focused on what other people think than on your own well-being. All I'm saying is that we have 60,000 thoughts a day, man. How are we supposed to keep up? The answer is we can't. We get overwhelmed. We need to create some space in there, and I'm serious, a little stillness and quiet will go a long way."

Sensing Isaac's patience running low, Gage demonstrated a couple of other simple breathing and relaxation techniques that had helped him in his own life, and encouraged Isaac to try them out sometime on his own.

Two weeks later, Isaac took an afternoon walk around the city. He found an opening in a fence that read "Meditation Gardens," and decided to take a look. The place had a hushed tone, and several other people walked in before him. As soon as he entered the gates, he followed a path of stone steps leading up into a huge, lush garden. There were succulent plants and hanging plants, and even a goldfish pond. Every so often, he saw a bench, some with people meditating.

He continued to make his way through the garden, exchanging smiles with other people and sinking into the quiet of the moment. He came upon a vacant bench that overlooked the ocean. He could see that he was up the beach from Gage's place, only much higher up on a large cliff overlooking the ocean. The surfers looked tiny, and the waves looked very different from this angle. He could see their full length from there, and the dynamic way they formed, crashed on the beach, and then rippled back out.

He closed his eyes and took a deep breath. Then another. Immediately his mind started imagining what he needed to do later, and then he began wondering about how long he would be here, and a host of other thoughts raced to the surface. He continued to breathe, and heard a seagull. He focused on that sound, and then, as if the volume had been turned up suddenly, he could hear only the roar of the ocean below. How had he not noticed it a few moments before? He let himself focus on the water, and the wind brushing through the nearby trees.

Isaac felt himself drifting off, and then opened his eyes. He looked around. How long have I been sitting here? But he felt extremely relaxed and at peace as he made his way back to Gage and Sharon's place.

Isaac was out again in the water the next morning. He still would not call himself a surfer, but he had certainly gained more balance on the board. A nice-sized wave rolled in. He jumped up into position, and found his center. He was surfing! The moment lasted almost 10 seconds, as he laughed out loud and drew closer to the shore. He was standing above it all, smoothly gliding through the froth. As he jumped off the board and into the shallow water near the beach, he noticed Gage yelling, giving him a big thumbs-up, and waving him over.

Isaac ran over, smiling and exhilarated. "That was sweet, man!" Gage beamed. "You did it!"

They walked together back over to the surf tent, and sat down. Isaac pulled out his water bottle and Gage peeled an orange. No customers in sight.

"So, do you mind if I share some more of my story with you, Isaac?"

Isaac was surprised that Gage even had to ask. "Of course—go ahead."

"Cool, thanks… So, here's my philosophy, and maybe you will get something out of it...

"I told you I went through some tough stuff. We all do, some more than others. But the point is that life will always be there to present challenges and problems. I can see now that I needed those things in order to move forward, and instead of problems, I now see them as opportunities. My higher power was watching over me the whole time, allowing me to keep learning and growing. For me, I couldn't see any of this until I got into meditation and prayer. Until I connected with that mysterious intelligent force that created all this." Gage nodded toward the ocean.

"When that negative voice in my head wouldn't stop and the past would haunt me, I had to turn it over to someone," he went on. "By seeking gratitude for all the blessings in my life, I switched up the energy flow and pulled away from such strong anger and resentment. Not just at others, but at myself.

"If you think that all this is a coincidence, then I think you're missing the bigger picture," Gage continued. "There are no accidents. You were meant to struggle and fall down so you could humble yourself and start to seek the answers. The key didn't come to you randomly. There is purpose behind all of it. Life is leading you somewhere."

At that moment, Gage stood up, put his hand out to help Isaac up, and said, "It's time. Can I see the key?"

Isaac pulled it from his backpack and handed it over. Gage stared down at the key, smiling and turning in his fingers a little ball bearing that looked like two beads welded together.

Gage led Isaac up the stairs to a room in the front of the house. He pushed aside a couple of surfboards and exposed an old wooden box. He pulled out a set of meditation beads and handed them to Isaac.

"These beads remind me of a time when I needed them the most. It is my role to tell you that this journey Mac sent you on is almost over. I'm the last 'stop' on the ride. It's all up to you now, and I hope these beads will lead you to as much peace as they did for me. Oh, and this is for you, too." He handed Isaac a small pocket-sized book called Tao Te Ching.

That night, Gage and Sharon took Isaac to a local seafood restaurant, and thanked him for all his help, inviting him to come back and visit anytime. The very next day, Isaac took a shuttle to the airport, and headed back to Chicago. He waited several hours to finally unfold Gage's note, trying to savor what he imagined would be a touching message:

Dear Isaac,

I know what it's like to be angry at yourself, angry at the world. All I can say is, spend as much time looking within as you do looking without. And remember that when you can see your darkness, you can learn to see your light.

-Gage

Resolution

By the time Isaac landed in Chicago and walked through the terminal, he realized he had not seen Amy for a few months. He had missed her terribly.

Sure enough, she was standing there with a sign, beaming and as beautiful as ever. But as a joke, she wrote out only his initials instead of his whole name. Her handwriting had left a large space between the first initial and the second two, so it read like this: "I. A.M."

Amy ran the last 10 steps and threw her arms around him in a tight embrace. "Isaac," she breathed happily. But rather than offering just a polite smile, Isaac felt confident yet emotional, holding her shoulders and looking deep into her eyes. "I missed you, too, Amy. Very much." He kissed her warmly, for the first time.

They grabbed his bags and walked together toward the parking garage.

For the next few months, Isaac fell into a comfortable schedule of working at the restaurant and spending time with Amy. He did a great deal of soul searching, processing all he had learned from his mentors. He also wrote letters to 12 people in his life, including his mother. It was time to heal old wounds.

It was also time to add his own section to the key, and become the latest member of that special brotherhood. To his surprise, though, after all he had been through and accomplished, he still felt a lot of self-doubt. Learning from his mentors had been amazing, but now he had to integrate everything into his actual, everyday life. It was time to walk the talk. What if I let them all down? What if the past comes back to haunt me?

He discussed his feelings with Amy at dinner one night, and wondered how he was supposed to suddenly become like Mac, Vick, Hugo, Dr. Ricardo, Chad, Charlie, Gage, and all the other people he had met and learned from.

Always wise and centered, Amy smiled. "You don't have to be like them, Isaac. You just have to be you."

After dinner, they caught a movie, but Isaac was lost in thought the whole time. As they walked back to the car, the whole adventure and Isaac's previous life of drug abuse and self-abuse seemed like a distant dream.

This was his new reality, the one he was creating. Amy stopped to look into a store window and Isaac followed her gaze. Isaac's eyes shifted focus from the mannequin in the window and his own reflection. It was foggy, and he could see cars and lights and other people passing through his reflection. He had to squint to see himself.

In a moment of profound clarity, he understood that life was still teaching him, even in that very moment. He was so caught up in worrying about the key, thinking about the past and the future, but missing the moments before him. As the cars continued to slide past behind him, he understood that past and future were created in the mind's eye, obscured by memories and perceived pain. Fuzzy and hard to focus, like the reflection in a store window.

Memory is when we create knowledge, like learning boundaries and recognizing limitations, Isaac realized. Imagination is where we create vision and the ability to see ourselves breaking through obstacles. But Isaac had been misusing his imagination to relive the pains and hurts of the past, to be a victim of his own story, instead of using it to learn and grow and forge a clear, healthy vision for the future.

Resolution comes when we pull ourselves from the window, into the body we inhabit, becoming honest in our view of ourselves. And honesty requires acceptance and removal of expectations, eliminating the need to be right and the fear of being wrong in the eyes of others. Resolution means finding ourselves, creating balance between past and future, reconciling thought and memory, surfing smoothly through the endless ocean of chaos and control.

Even as the storm raged within, he knew that he could still find that stillness, that peace, calm, and confidence that come from deep inside. His mentors had taught him that, and now he had a mountain of evidence to pull from.

Isaac's thoughts were swirling, but he felt connected and grounded as he continued to stare into the window and hold Amy's hand. He smiled with the memories and of how far he had come.

Amy was right, he thought. My name is Isaac Adam McFarland, I. A.M. And that's enough.

He had certainly done things worth writing about, and felt that maybe, just maybe, he could share it in a way that people would enjoy reading.

A month later, Isaac took a long weekend off from the restaurant, and went to visit his mother. For the first time in his adult life, he spoke openly to her about his feelings. Before long, he was crying and apologizing, and leaning into her gentle embrace.

He looked into her eyes and explained how much he had blamed her for his own inner turmoil and for his father leaving...How much he had blamed his family for setting healthy boundaries with him when he had become toxic and abusive... How much he beat himself up inside and sabotaged so many jobs and relationships.

Isaac asked for her forgiveness, which she willingly gave. For a long time, he sat next to his mom and held her hand, and they both cried as he thanked her over and over for everything she had done for him.

Next, Isaac went back to the farm to visit Mac. They were sitting on the back porch, and Isaac was holding the key, looking down at the new section. He ran his piece in between his fingers. It had taken him a lot of thought to finally be able to choose his piece of the key. He had gone back and forth for weeks, but finally found the perfect thing.

It was a gold coin about the size of a nickel. The word "Recovery" was etched on one side, and "To Thy Own Self Be True" on the other. As he reread each phrase, he choked up a bit with pride and gratitude.
Isaac looked up and caught Mac staring back at him.

"How did you come about choosing your piece?" Mac asked curiously.

"It's my one-year sobriety chip. I had it sized down in order for it to fit just right," Isaac chuckled. "I felt that it represented my journey and everything that I have learned along the way perfectly."

Isaac leaned forward in his chair toward Mac, finally asking the question that had been running continually in his head for months. "How did you know?

"What do you mean?" Mac asked with a bit of a twinkle in his eye.

"You told me that when I was a small boy, you saw it in my eyes that I would be the 'one.' How did you know?"

Mac settled deeper into his chair. "Well, ever since you were a small boy, you have been very defiant. I learned a long time ago that those who are defiant become determined when they finally get that fire in their belly. And I knew that would eventually happen for you, when defiance became determination, and determination would turn into tenacity—the ability to do whatever it takes to get the answer you have been looking for."

Isaac felt the truth in Mac's words and looked deep into his grandfather's eyes. "Thank you, Mac. Thanks for believing in me, even when I didn't."

Isaac then looked off into the distance, shaking his head and laughing a bit.

Mac noticed and said, "What's tickling you now?"

Isaac said, "It' just that I think I know who might be next."

He then stood up and leaned toward Mac, making it clear that he was initiating a hug. Mac stood, too, and they embraced quietly and knowingly for a full minute.

A decade later, Isaac and Amy had been married for eight years, and she was pregnant with their second child. They had bought the restaurant in Chicago when Vick's health began to fail.

One cold, rainy afternoon, just in the middle of the lunch rush, Amy was working the register and Isaac was on the grill. A young man waited patiently in line and then began speaking to Amy, who turned and caught Isaac's eye.

He watched the young man reach into his shirt and pull out a necklace with a key on it. Isaac could faintly hear him: "My name is Carlo. I am Paulo's son, Hugo's grandson. I was told to ask for Isaac."

Isaac walked around the counter and introduced himself. "Have a seat right over there, Carlo." He then turned to Amy and smiled. "Amy, would you be so kind as to grab us a couple of burgers?"

Learn More

———————————●●●———————————

TurningLeaf offers services for individuals and families in mental health, substance abuse, life coaching and personal development, as well as corporate training and personal growth seminars.

Visit www.TurningLeafWellnessCenter.com call (435) 652-1202 to learn more. It's not about change; it's about growth.

Lee Kelley Creative Group offers professional writing services including ghostwriting, creative collaboration, and book proposal development.

You can learn more at leekelley4.com or by calling (435) 272-4618.

Made in the USA
Monee, IL
17 April 2023

31994449R00059